Somewhere South

Somewhere South

Sailing Through Polynesia 1977

CLAY HUTCHINSON

ILLUSTRATIONS BY CLEMSON LAM

Somewhere South
Sailing Through Polynesia 1977

Edited by Jane Crosen
Design and composition by Claire MacMaster
barefoot art graphic design

Printed by Printworks Global Ltd., London & Hong Kong

First Edition

ISBN: 978-1-7325470-9-4

"When you come to a fork in the road, take it"

—YOGI BERRA

*"It seems to me that the natural world
is the greatest source of excitement;
the greatest source of visual beauty;
the greatest source of intellectual interest.
It is the greatest source of so much in life
that makes life worth living."*

—SIR DAVID FREDERICK ATTENBOROUGH

CONTENTS

PREFACE AND ACKNOWLEDGMENTS

THIS IS A MEMOIR that I have been writing in my head for over 40 years. I retired in 2016 and resumed Pacific Ocean sailing in earnest, making numerous long-distance voyages on my boat and friends' boats. When the Covid pandemic put my cruising life on hold, I finally sat down and put pen to paper. This story is taken from the entries in my 1977 logbook, augmented with additional memories of the voyage provided by my cousin and shipmate John Garth. Some of the names of the characters in the memoir have been changed to "protect the innocent."

I am forever grateful to my close friend Clemson Lam who interpreted my memoir and produced the vibrant watercolors and intriguing maps that bring the story to life.

My sailing buddies Fred Garth, Noodle Leary, Mark Logan, Roger Hammer, Craig Fostvedt, Doug Hiller, Bo Wheeler, Rob Barrel, Graham Kyd, and my son Jonathan all read the story and provided excellent technical comments as the manuscript evolved. Thanks Shipmates!

Maynard Bray of *WoodenBoat* magazine provided excellent advice about publishing and introduced me to Jane Crosen of Crackerjack Editorial Services. Jane approached the job with genuine interest and enthusiasm and patiently guided me through the editing process. Spencer Smith of Seapoint Books + Media willingly took on this novice author and assembled a top-notch team approach to publishing. In addition to Jane Crosen, Spencer's team included Claire MacMaster of Barefoot Art Graphic Design. It was a real pleasure working with Claire as she presented many creative ideas and solutions and got the job done well in minimum time.

I especially want to acknowledge the encouragement and guidance provided by my wife Gail and our daughter Grace Hall.

My first command, 1955

Finding *Lille Dansker*

Boats have always been a source of wonder for me. Every serious boater knows that a proper vessel is a work of art and mystery and something to be cherished.

My adventure began when my father put my hand on the tiller of a 2.5-horsepower Elgin outboard when I was five years old. That was in Soldier Creek, a bayou of Perdido Bay, Alabama. I knew immediately that boating was my destiny.

The motor was mounted to a 14-foot open flat-bottomed launch made from juniper wood (*Juniperus cupressaceae)* that had been harvested from the brackish-water bayous of Perdido Bay. The topsides of the boat were white, and the deck and interior were painted light green. She was a beauty.

Over the years, we had several small boats, and I spent countless hours driving, repairing, cleaning, and just sitting in them. My best childhood memories all involve boats. My father and I made a plywood Sailfish from a kit when I was six. My older brother Hank and I got a blunt-bowed 14-foot aluminum boat with a 9.9-horse Mercury when I was nine. That boat was feather light, dangerously unstable, and blazing fast, and we learned boat handling through trial and error, mostly error. We had a Snipe, a 14-foot centerboard sloop that was a great boat for learning the technical aspects of sailing.

In 1956 Dad purchased a 16-foot fiberglass-reinforced plastic (FRP) runabout with a 35-horse Johnson. That was in the early days of fiberglass construction, and the boat was built just like a wooden boat but with FRP ribs and stringers. The hull was laid up to appear to be lapstrake. She had a varnished mahogany foredeck that I refinished several times.

My uncle had lots of boats, the first of which was a juniper strip-planked 16-foot open runabout named *Greenie* with a 25-horse Johnson that ran—sometimes. It was pull-cranked and had wheel steering and lever shift and throttle. *Greenie* lived a full life and served admirably for many years, even venturing out into the Gulf of Mexico on fishing trips. She ended her life as an herb-garden vessel in the front yard, eventually decomposing back into the soil from whence she came.

Soldier Creek, Perdido Bay, Alabama, 1955

During college I started making plans for an open-ocean sailing voyage and read a lot of books on the subject, including books by Eric Hiscock, Francis Chichester, William Albert Robinson, and others. The writings of Eric Hiscock resonated with me. His practical approach to cruising with emphasis on proper yacht construction and maintenance just made sense, and I read and reread all his books.

I joined the Navy after college, spent a year in Naval Flight Officer training, and then received orders to a C-130 squadron in Hawaii.

Sailing opportunities in Hawaii were wide open, and I was able to find crew positions on several inter-island voyages. I also spent many hours walking the docks at Ala Wai Small Boat Harbor. Then one day *Lille Dansker* arrived from Tahiti, after sailing down the West Coast of the U.S. to Mexico, out to the Marquesas, and then through the Tuamotus and Society Islands. I was immediately taken by the boat, asked permission to board, and talked for several hours with the owner. It was probably obvious to him that I was hooked.

I could not afford to buy the boat by myself, so convinced a Navy buddy from my squadron and two Army doctors to buy the boat with me as a four-way partnership. We moved the boat to Rainbow Bay Marina in Pearl Harbor and made lots of very pleasant sails out of the harbor and up to Diamond Head.

When we started venturing outside of Oahu's protected waters, the other owners gradually decided that sailing offshore in Hawaiian waters was not exactly comfortable. To be fair, we did blow out the main during an aborted sail to Maui, and that convinced the others.

As I gained experience aboard *Lille Dansker*, the dream of voyaging somewhere faraway in the Pacific began to develop and solidify in my mind. *Lille Dansker* had made many ocean passages and was clearly capable of making more. I realized that with more experience I could be ready for a real adventure aboard a fine vessel.

I talked my cousin John Garth into going in 50/50 with me on the boat. John grew up on boats on Perdido Bay and the Gulf of Mexico and was completely comfortable out in the Blue. John was a natural around boats, a good fisherman, and loved the ocean. Both of us had some experience working on tugboats during college summers.

John had just graduated from college and moved to Hawaii to hang out with me before returning to the mainland for graduate school. He initially took a job picking pineapples, before moving up to a job as a Fuller Brush salesman. He was not exactly making a killing, and the idea of going sailing across the Pacific was intriguing.

When I finished the active-duty portion of my Navy obligation in February 1977, we went to work full time getting the boat ready to head South. We sailed around to Kaneohe Bay and rented a slip at Makani Kai Marina. Despite our extensive powerboating experience, we were not sailors, and we did some incredibly stupid things as we learned to handle the boat.

We made two voyages to Maui with a crowd of mostly total novices. Roger, a Navy buddy, was aboard for the first trip. He had his own boat and had made the voyage to Maui the year before. Roger's experience was a big help. On the first trip, I decided that leaving at midnight during a moderate gale was a great idea. As it turned out, it was a terrible idea but was also the most fun I had ever had to that point, and we were fortunate to arrive at Kamalapau Harbor, Lanai, with all hands still aboard and alive. Being young and stupid has some advantages.

One of the young women aboard had grown up on Lanai, so we all got a ride up to Lanai City and spent the night in her parents' house, sprawled out on the floor and couches. Her father played guitar and sang Hawaiian songs well into the early hours.

Although most of the crew had been miserably seasick en route to Lanai, they hung with us as we continued to Maui, Molokai, and then home to Oahu. We had a good time in Lahaina…hard not to have a good time in Lahaina. We anchored in Honolua Bay, Maui, for a few nights and then sailed down to Kaunakakai Harbor on the south shore of Molokai.

We met a man named Kamuela on the pier and asked him to recommend a good place to hike, and he told us about Halawa Valley and then offered to take us there. He said he had not visited the valley in several years and needed a break anyway.

Fred, Robert, Clay, and John—the cousins on the north shore of Molokai, 1977

Molokai Island north shore

Kamuela had a large cargo van, so we all piled in and made the long drive to the east end of the island, walked into the valley, and ran into a group of free-spirited folks dancing naked around a fire pit singing the songs from *Hair*. There was this one wild-haired little fellow named Willy who was super friendly and talkative. He reminded me of Cousin It from the Addams Family. His girlfriend Moonglow was about twice his size. Willy told us he had downed "copious quantities" of coffee so far that morning. He said that it was part of his daily routine to get wired on coffee and then dance.

The whole naked group offered to lead us up to the falls at the head of the valley. It was a little disconcerting walking behind the behinds of a bunch of wired naked people, but the waterfall was gorgeous, and we had a wonderful hike.

Back at the campsite, Willy stoked the fire, while talking staccato about everything. He had been living unclothed in the valley for six months and said it was good to meet some folks from the "World." As he talked, he tended the fire by picking up red-hot embers with his bare hands. Don't ask me how that is possible. Maybe it is something like walking on red-hot coals. I don't have a clue how he did that without getting burned.

Ha'upu Bay, Molokai Island

We talked a bit about our sailing trip, and when we said that we had to get moving because it was getting dark, Willy spoke right up and asked if he could go on the boat with us to Honolulu. John and I talked briefly and asked Kamuela, who said okay to adding another passenger in the van. I then told Willy that he could go with us on the conditions that he wear some clothes and must have money to take care of himself in Honolulu and then get back to Molokai. Willy asked if we had coffee onboard and when we said yes, he ran into the bushes and emerged soon thereafter wearing a shirt and long pants and carrying a full duffel bag. He kissed Moonglow goodbye and bounded out towards the van. He had no shoes.

Willy turned out to be an unusually pleasant, intelligent, funny, and interesting character, and he was an excellent deckhand. He enjoyed every minute of sailing and living aboard the boat for a few weeks in Honolulu, and was always upbeat and ready to tackle any job. Since he had not been indoors for many months, he preferred to sleep in the cockpit. He made a bit of cash working on other boats in the harbor and quickly became friends with nearby boat owners. He had good mechanical skills and completed a thorough inspection of our engine, followed by a good engine cleaning and painting. His diminutive size paid off when working in tight spots on the boat.

The second voyage to Maui was much the same, with some great sailing and a few near disasters. John's brother Fred was with us along with another cousin, Robert, and our friend Marc Carter, all very experienced on the water.

We anchored in Ha'upu Bay on the north shore of Molokai by tying our anchor chain around a boulder in 40 feet of water. Yeah, we really did that. We did not have scuba gear aboard and had to free-dive to tie and untie.

From Ha'upu Bay we sailed a few miles west down the coast and anchored (with a real anchor) in the sand bottom at Kalaupapa in the lee of the peninsula. We paddled our dinghy close to the town dock and held position as we spoke with a gentleman on the dock, eventually receiving an invitation for all hands to come ashore. As it turned out, the gentleman was the town sheriff, a very kind and interesting man. He escorted us for a walking tour of the village, the last stop being the village tavern. We had a few beers with the sheriff and met lots of wonderful folks.

Kalaupapa was established in the 1870s as a quarantine village for victims of Hansen's disease (leprosy), at one time being the home for 1,200 patients. We were fortunate to be invited ashore at this beautiful place. The peninsula was closed to outsiders except by invitation, and is now preserved as the Kalaupapa National Historical Park.

We sailed home to Oahu and when we got back to the marina in Kaneohe Bay, John, Marc, and I spent the evening discussing the high points of the trip. It had been Marc's first time on a sailboat, and it was obvious that he had loved every minute.

Marc was a quiet and modest person, and we were stunned when after a couple of beers, he asked if he could join as crew for the sail to Tahiti. We just smiled and toasted our new shipmate. At the time Marc was completing a machinist apprenticeship in Honolulu, having spent four years in the Navy as a diver with a UDT command (Underwater Demolition Team).

Marc had excellent mechanical skills, spent every weekend jumping out of perfectly good airplanes, loved being on and under the ocean, and wanted to have some fun before settling down to a full-time job. He was an interesting and enthusiastic person, and on top of all that, we learned in the coming months that Marc was totally fearless. Granted, having been a UDT diver meant that he had to be very tough, but fearlessness is not learned; it is or is not part of one's being. That attribute came to the fore on several occasions during the voyage.

Lille Dansker, 1947

The Boat

JOHN AND I considered ownership of *Lille Dansker* to be an honor and a very serious responsibility. She had an impeccable pedigree and we recognized that we were guardians of a work of art. Boats like *Lille Dansker* are rare indeed. She was designed by Aage Nielsen and Murray Peterson as a gaff-rigged ketch and built by Hodgdon Bros. in East Boothbay, Maine, in 1947.

Mr. Nielsen based the hull design on Denmark's *toldkrdser* (toll cruiser) revenue cutters. The name *Lille Dansker* translates to "Little Dane." Mr. Peterson designed the rig and arrangements. The result was a proper yacht that had the appearance of a little ship.

Knud Aage Nielsen

Lille Dansker, the little ship in 1947

Lille Dansker's displacement was 33,920 pounds, of which 10,000 pounds were in the lead keel. She had white oak (*Quercus alba*) framing, longleaf pine planking, and 1¾-inch teak decks. Spars were made from Port Orford cedar. Exterior trim was mahogany and teak. The interior was black walnut. While the above-water appearance was typical of Danish revenue cutters, Nielsen designed a more modern underbody that proved to be very slippery and left almost no wake.

For a description of the deck layout and rig, I will start at the bow and work aft. The club-footed, self-tending jibboom was attached to the cranse at the tip of the bowsprit. Wire rope whisker stays led from the cranse to port and starboard catheads, which had internal rollers for hoisting and stowing anchors. The bobstay was also wire rope. There was no dolphin striker. A web of soft-line safety netting was slung beneath the bowsprit and secured to the whisker stays. The jibstay ran to the top of the mainmast, and the headstay ran to the top of the main topmast.

LILLE DANSKER
KAN design 105
(Peterson design 149) of 1947

LOA 38'8"
LWL 35'10"
Beam 11'10"
Draft 5'9"
Sail Area 855 sq ft

Lille Dansker as featured in *WoodenBoat* magazine, 1996

The jibboom had a four-part sheet that led through a series of blocks down to the foredeck and could be led aft. There were beefy hawsepipes in the bow. Just aft of the stem was a very stout oak samson post mounted through the deck into the chain locker. Aft of that was the Ideal electric anchor windlass, a bronze monster with twin gypsies that fed into the chain locker. The chain locker was huge and had an 18-inch-diameter round locking manhole cover. You are probably getting the picture that *Lille* was a proper little ship.

The cabin trunk had a nice mahogany opening skylight. The sliding companionway hatch was mahogany, and there were vertically mounted hinged mahogany doors leading down into the cabin. Dorade ventilators were positioned over the chain locker, main cabin, 'midship cabin, and engine room. Side decks provided about 2½ feet of clearance between the cabin trunk and bulwarks. A beefy hand-operated bilge pump was mounted through the deck 'midships on the port side. Since it didn't require electrical power and provided a good physical workout, it became our primary bilge pump.

Our most important pre-departure project was taking *Lille* to dry-dock. In 1977 Hawaiian Tuna Packers in Kewalo Basin, Honolulu, was a very good dry-dock facility. I had taken *Lille* there for routine haulouts on two previous occasions, and this time we needed to pull the rudder, change the depthsounder transducer and two through-hull fittings, and then antifoul the bottom before departing for the South Pacific.

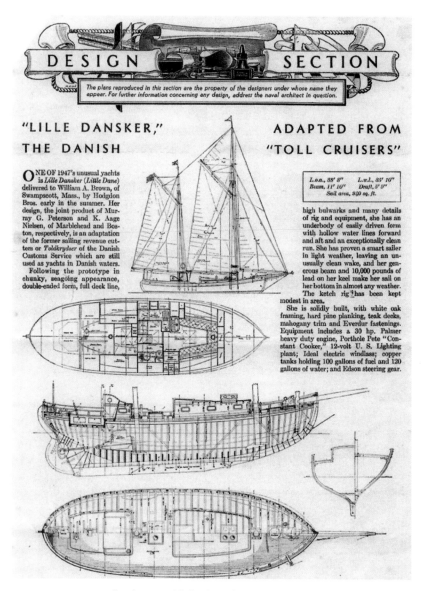

"LILLE DANSKER," THE DANISH

ADAPTED FROM "TOLL CRUISERS"

ONE OF 1947's unusual yachts is *Lille Dansker* (*Little Dane*) delivered to William A. Brown, of Swampscott, Mass., by Hodgdon Bros. early in the summer. Her design, the joint product of Murray G. Peterson and K. Aage Nielsen, of Marblehead and Boston, respectively, is an adaptation of the former sailing revenue cutters or *Toldkrydser* of the Danish Customs Service which are still used as yachts in Danish waters.

Following the prototype in chunky, seagoing appearance, double-ended form, full deck line,

L.o.a., 38' 8"	L.w.l., 35' 10"
Beam, 11' 10"	Draft, 5' 5"
Sail area, 950 sq. ft.	

high bulwarks and many details of rig and equipment, she has an underbody of easily driven form with hollow water lines forward and aft and an exceptionally clean run. She has proven a smart sailer in light weather, leaving an unusually clean wake, and her generous beam and 10,000 pounds of lead on her keel make her sail on her bottom in almost any weather.

The ketch rig has been kept modest in area.

She is solidly built, with white oak framing, hard pine planking, teak decks, mahogany trim and Everdur fastenings. Equipment includes a 30 hp. Palmer heavy duty engine, Porthole Pete "Constant Cooker," 12-volt U. S. Lighting plant; Ideal electric windlass; copper tanks holding 100 gallons of fuel and 120 gallons of water; and Edson steering gear.

Lille's lines published in *The Rudder*, 1947

Hawaiian Tuna Packers was established in the early 20th century to service the fleet of wooden Hawaiian fishing sampans, known as "*aku* boats." The sampan design was based on the vessels of the Japanese fishing fleet and had been modified for rougher Hawaiian waters. The rugged, functionally beautiful boats were manned by hardworking, very tough and gnarly crew. The shipyard was staffed by highly skilled old-school shipwrights. Haulout was accomplished with a marine

"LILLE DANSKER"

ONE of the most colorful yachts to be built since the war, *Lille Dansker* is an adaptation of the former Danish revenue cutters, or "Toldkrydser." She was designed by Murray G. Peterson and K. Aage Nielsen for W. A. Brown, of Swampscott, Mass., and built by Hodgdon Bros. Her auxiliary is a 30 hp. Palmer heavy duty engine.

Douglas Photo Shop photos

She follows the prototype in chunky, seagoing appearance, double-ended form

Her dimensions are: 38'8" l.o.a., 35'10" l.w.l., 11' 10" beam and 5'9" draft. Sail area is 940 sq. ft.

"Lille Dansker" was designed for comfort, and the snowshoe type helmsman's seat (right) is typical of her cockpit

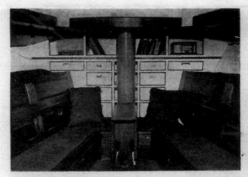

Her forward cabin sleeps four, and is spacious enough to be the center of activities below. Note the drawers in the forward bulkhead

She is solidly built, with white oak framing, hard pine planking, teak decks and mahogany trim

These two views of her cabin are characteristic of her many unusual details. Basic equipment, however, is most modern

Lille featured as a newly launched vessel in *The Rudder,* 1947

railway/diesel engine driven winch system. Prior to hauling the boat up the railway, skin-divers dove under the boat in fish offal–filled water to place cradle alignment dunnage. Just watching the process was an impressive experience. When the divers signaled that all was ready, the winch was engaged, and the boat was hauled up the rails to a turntable up on the flat of the yard and then moved along a spur to the working position in the yard. Once in position, the cradle was replaced with jack-screw supports.

Soon after hauling the boat, we found that we had a soft plank on the starboard side. I knew that our limited carpentry skills did not include cutting, shaping, steaming, and bending a 1½-inch-thick compound curved plank, so we met with the shipyard manager. He summoned his master shipwright, a small wiry character who bounded up the ladder to examine the plank for a few minutes and then disappeared into the shop without a word.

I asked the shipyard manager if he had any 1½-inch-thick yellow pine planking. He responded that he would search, and then recommended that we not worry about the plank and instead go to work on pulling the rudder.

The master returned with a small three-legged stool, sat down, and proceeded to stare at the boat for about 10 minutes. He then vanished into the shop with his stool.

The next morning, we arrived at 0700 to find that the master had already removed the bad plank and was making the initial fit-up of the new one. He made a few pencil marks, removed the plank, and took it back to the shop. I never once saw him take any measurements. After a couple of minor adjustments, the plank fit perfectly and was installed with fasteners made of Monel, a nickel-copper alloy.

John and I started caulking the seams until the master shipwright, without speaking, took the mallet and caulking iron from me and then demonstrated how it should be done. Like most technical jobs, there is science and a bit of art to caulking a seam, and we did a commendable job. The seam never leaked, so Bob's your uncle.

As we proceeded with the rudder work, a sailor who was working on his boat stopped by to talk and asked if we were planning to pull the worm shoe. Rather than broadcast my ignorance, I said, "Haven't decided yet," after which the fellow kneeled down, put his head underneath the keel just forward of the rudder, and then said, "Looks pretty sound, but I recommend you pull it just to be sure." John nodded in agreement, "Yeah, you are probably right, can't be too careful."

Later that day we got out our brace with a flat-head screwdriver bit and removed the eight Everdur (silicon-bronze) screws holding the worm shoe to the deadwood. When the last of the screws let go, the worm shoe fell hard to the concrete with a resounding clang, like steel on steel. I said, "What the hell is that thing?" The yard manager happened to be walking past and said, "That worm shoe is made from lignum vitae wood, and it is the heaviest and hardest wood in the world. That worm shoe is so hard that worms can't eat it, and it prevents them from eating into the main structure of the boat."

He examined the board and declared that it was as good as new and then recommended reinstalling it with a generous bedding of Git-Rot sealant and new fasteners.

I went to the library (this was before that know-it-all Siri became the world's authority on just about everything) to read about lignum vitae and learned, among other interesting facts, that it weighs 84 pounds per cubic foot. The worm shoe was about 4 feet long, 10 inches wide, and 3 inches thick, meaning that it weighed about 70 pounds. For comparison, longleaf yellow pine weighs about 41 pounds per cubic foot, and white oak weighs about 47 pounds per cubic foot.

It dawned on me that there were other items on the boat that had the same lignum vitae dark olive color, including the deadeyes and the belaying pins. Examination revealed that they were indeed made of lignum vitae.

John and Clay on departure day

3

Casting Off the Lines

TYPICAL OF MOST SAILORS preparing for their first extended voyage, we underestimated the amount of work needed to prepare for departure. One of the big voyage preparation jobs was recaulking the teak deck. Some of the seams were leaking. We used a dado blade to cut out the old sealant, reefed out and replaced the cotton caulking and oakum, and resealed the seams with Thiokol, a flexible polysulfide polymer. We also removed and replaced all the old teak plugs. We finished the job by belt-sanding the deck, which looked new at completion of the job. The seams did not leak.

Throwing off the docklines is the hardest part of any sailing adventure. You are never completely ready, and there is always an excuse to do one more chore. Perhaps it is the subconscious fear of the unknown that makes that task so difficult. But, once out to sea, it gets easy. Like a lot of situations in life, you just have to cast off and go for it.

We planned to sail Somewhere South and had hoped to depart from Hawaii in May but were not ready until the first week of July. The last few weeks went by in a blur of endless seemingly crucial jobs.

During the last of the preparations, we were worn out and just had to take a break, so John and I went to a July 4th party at a friend's house where we expected to meet up with Marc and his skydiving buddies. The host was roasting a pig in an *imu* (in-ground fire pit), and suddenly a young woman looked up and shrieked, "Oh my God!" Right then Marc and another skydiver landed right in the fire pit, wearing nothing but jump boots, jock straps, and parachutes. They emerged only slightly singed and were handed cold Primo beers, the local favorite. Now that was an original and proper entrance.

"Stand first to the N of the Hawaiian Islands, and then make easting in the Northeast Trade, cross the equator well to the E, and then proceed SW in the South-east Trade to Tahiti."

These are the words posted in the 1973 edition of *Ocean Passages for the World* for the recommended sailing route from Hawaii to Tahiti. We were novices and needed all the advice we could get. Early on I studied the recommendation and plotted a course accordingly.

Soon thereafter, poring over the charts and hoisting a few beers with some experienced sailors, we were advised to ignore the *Ocean Passages* advice and instead sail southeast from Honolulu in the lee of the islands. They recommended that we set a waypoint of 10 degrees north latitude, 147 degrees west longitude after rounding South Point on Hawaii Island (the Big Island). The reasoning was that by following the leeward route we would have a more comfortable departure and we should still be able to make enough easting prior to reaching the Intertropical Convergence Zone (ITCZ), followed by the southeast trade winds. Also, sailing a-lee of the islands would provide a good shakedown and avoid several days of pounding right into the typically strong trades and associated seas to the east of the island chain.

The Polynesian voyaging canoe *Hokulea* had taken the route to weather of the islands the year before in 1976 and had gotten hammered for several days trying to gain easting. So, we decided it would be prudent to just head southeast and take our chances.

We completed the last of the to-do list and then spent a couple of days provisioning, which mostly consisted of canned food, potatoes, onions, oranges, grapefruit, canned juices, rice, Bisquick, coffee, plastic milk (powdered milk), and so on. None of us could be considered decent cooks, so it would have been a waste to bring more expensive foods. We were prepared to subsist on cheap canned peas and carrots, peanut butter & jelly sandwiches, canned tuna, and rather disgusting canned whole chicken. We did bring a lot of won bok cabbage, which we were told would last several weeks. It turned out to be a mainstay when slathered with peanut butter.

John surprised us with a whole case of canned sardines. Now, I like sardines, and one or two now and then is plenty. But the case of sardines turned out to be our best bartering tool. The islanders loved canned sardines, and trading one can would yield a stalk of bananas or several papayas or a multitude of other delicious fruits.

I made the mistake of buying a full case of almost-ripe tomatoes, which decided to go off within days of departure and shortly thereafter spontaneously combusted in the storage cabinet and drained into the bilge, resulting in an almost edible tomato-puree bilgewater soup. Had the combustion happened later in the voyage, we might have considered the soup for a main course.

Several friends saw us off at the marina and things got a bit too emotional, with lots of "Call us on the radio, send a card from Tahiti, promise to come home, etc." So, draped with flower *lei*, we threw off the lines at 1230 and motored out into Kaneohe Bay.

We had stowed cases and cases of canned food in John's bunk, which was on the port side in the 'midship cabin. The cases were lashed in with a lee cloth and John's mattress was rigged on top of the canned food. The weight of the canned food gave us a pronounced port list, which was okay since we expected to be on port tack for most of the trip south and having the extra weight on the port side would help to keep the boat upright.

We hoisted the main and mizzen with single reefs and the working jib, and motor-sailed out of the Sampan Channel into a nice 15–18-knot trade wind. I was completely exhausted, having been working 18–20-hour days in recent weeks dealing with last-minute details. The relief of finally getting underway was massive. I think John and Marc felt the same. Now all we had to do was take care of the boat, and she would take care of us. Voyaging is just that simple.

Once well clear of the Sampan Channel we tacked onto port, cleared through the gap between Mokapu Point and Moku Manu Island, and headed across the Kaiwi Channel to Molokai Island. The trade winds provided a good point of sail, and we had no trouble laying La'au Point on the southwestern tip of Molokai.

The wind got up that night as we sailed across the Kalohi Channel between Molokai and Lanai, and we started taking on a lot of water down the decks and into the cockpit. That was when we learned that we had neglected to properly seal the lazarette hatches in the cockpit—one of those jobs that just did not get done. The hatches were made into the sidewalls of the cockpit well and were awash whenever a slug of water flowed down the deck into the cockpit, so a proper seal was mandatory.

Contributing to the problem was the weight we were carrying. We were stocked with several months' supply of food and had not adequately considered how that would affect trim, performance, and seakeeping. In addition, we were carrying 300 feet of ⅜-inch chain in the chain locker forward. So, we decided to pull into Hulapoe Bay on the lee side of the island of Lanai and anchor for a day. We were in no rush and needed the rest anyway. We slept soundly that afternoon and through the night. Hulapoe Bay was a legal anchorage in those days, a beautiful, sheltered bay with crystal-clear water and a hard white sand bottom.

We made the lazarette seal repairs, shifted the anchor chain into the 'midship bilge, and headed back out, keeping Kahoolawe Island to port.

The Alenuihaha, the channel between Maui and the Big Island, is 25 nautical miles wide at the narrowest point. The high mountains on Maui and the Big Island funnel the wind down the channel, resulting in a venturi that can produce legendary winds and seas. The English translation of the Hawaiian word *Alenuihaha* is "Great billows smashing." By keeping Kahoolawe Island to port and then sailing directly for the Kona coast, we would be crossing the channel as it opened to about 50 nautical miles wide. This was our first Alenuihaha crossing, and we had been told by an experienced sailor to keep the wind on the beam and that we would eventually get lifted into the lee of the Big Island after crossing the channel.

Crossing that far down and thus avoiding the narrow and windy portion of the channel was a good call. I had heard the Alenuihaha horror stories of 15–20-foot seas and 30–40-knot winds on the good days, but as it turned out we had a glorious nighttime beam reach. Around midnight, confronting gusts to 35 knots, we doused the main and sailed with working jib and single-reefed mizzen, a configuration that sounds odd, but the boat was balanced and comfortable. *Lille* steered herself most of the way across. We just had to trim the mizzen to act as the rudder and then lash the helm. That is the beauty of a ketch rig, lots of options. We were not sailing fast, but we were comfortable. *Lille* did not have a wind vane or an autopilot.

About dawn we did get lifted into the light winds of the huge Big Island lee. There are few vistas more stunning than sunrise over Hualalai and Mauna Loa mountains from offshore the Kona coast.

We spent the daylight hours easing our way south down the Kona coast in near-flat seas, taking that opportunity to stow gear that had come adrift, cleaning the bilge of the tomato-puree "soup," and stuffing rags and sponges in cabinets to silence pots, pans, and general stuff. Having those last couple of days to fine-tune the boat before hitting open water was a huge help.

The boat was squared away by the time we were abeam Kealakekua Bay, so we decided to drop sails and go for a swim. Like I said, we were not in a hurry. That was very refreshing.

After the swim I took a few minutes to start my logbook for the voyage. It was then that I realized that we had departed Kaneohe on 7/7/77. We had been so focused on leaving that we hadn't noticed the significance of the date. It was most definitely good karma. Our logbook was hardbound and canvas-covered with heavy blank paper pages.

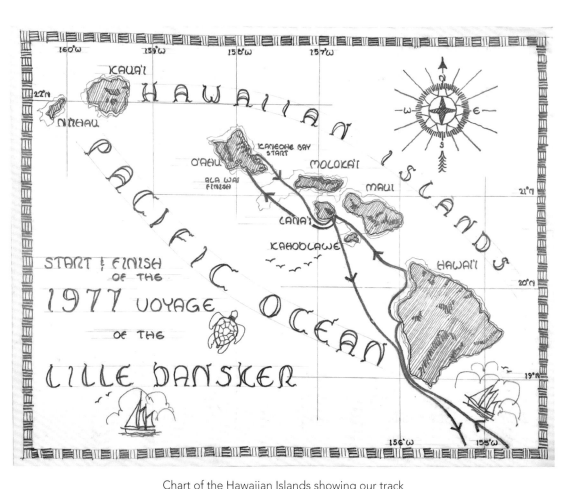

Chart of the Hawaiian Islands showing our track

4

Into the Big Blue

THE NORTHEAST TRADE WINDS wrap around South Point of the Big Island, so later that evening we closed with the shore for the last 20 miles or so to get a bit of a lee and then close-reached to South Point which was abeam at about midnight. As expected, the seas increased dramatically once we cleared South Point, but the point of sail was good, and we were able to sail in relative comfort.

I was on watch at sunrise as the Big Island sank into the sea. That was when I knew that we were really and truly on our way to Somewhere South. I spoke with *Lille* and told her that I would do everything within my abilities to help her get us somewhere safely. She just sighed and surged ahead.

When pressed, we had told friends and family that we were headed to Papeete, Tahiti, but we really weren't set on sailing to a particular island or group of islands. We just wanted to go Somewhere South, and the voyage was the destination. We had, however, met with the French Consulate in Honolulu to ascertain that we met the requirements for entry into French Polynesia.

Leaving the Big Island astern and heading out into the Big Blue was a life-changing experience. Suddenly, we were totally on our own. What a magnificent feeling. There was no turning back. We were focused on the sea miles ahead, and looking back meant nothing. Everything worth considering was forward of *Lille*'s bow. John and Marc must have sensed that something profound was happening, or maybe I let out a hoot, but anyway they woke up, came topside, looked astern briefly, and then turned to gaze forward with huge smiles on their faces. No words were spoken, but we knew that we had some great adventures ahead. A quote from Jacques Cousteau's beautiful book *The Silent World* is appropriate here:

> *"Sometimes we are lucky enough to know that our lives have been changed to discard the old, embrace the new, and run headlong down an immutable course...."*

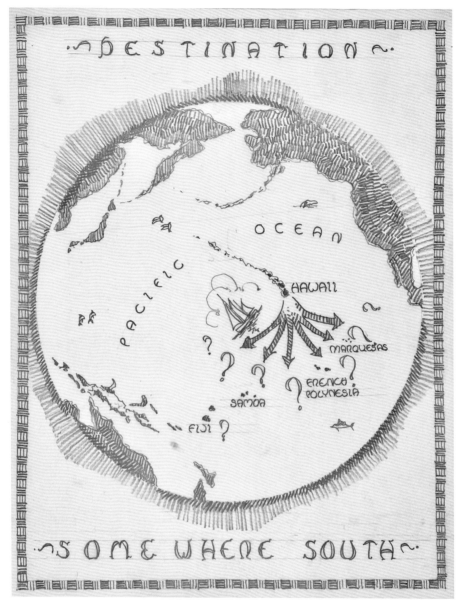

Our planned route to Somewhere South

The seas within 50 miles or so of the Big Island were confused and lumpy due to all that enhanced wind, current, and seas being forced to go around the island, and it was not until the afternoon that the sea settled into a nice, rolling rhythm.

The lee to the west of the Big Island can extend to more than 100 miles. Mauna Kea and Mauna Loa, the two highest mountains on the Big Island, are just shy of 14,000 feet, creating a barrier that forces the trade winds to turn either north or south to round the island. Fortunately, the mountains also serve to divert hurricanes that approach the Big Island, as hurricanes get their energy from the warm sea and cannot pass over the high mountains. If not for those mountains, the islands of Hawaii would be hit by hurricanes more frequently.

South Point is approximately 19 degrees north latitude, 155 degrees 40 minutes west longitude, so we needed to make good a true course of 136 degrees to reach our first waypoint at 10 north, 147 west. The trades were still favoring a bit north-northeast, so we were holding a good heading.

What I did not understand then was the impact of sailing too close to the wind and the resulting leeway, especially on a gaff-rigged ketch that was not known for windward performance. I put far too much emphasis on making the waypoint and not enough emphasis on boat speed. In hindsight, we should have trimmed the boat for speed, which would have resulted in less leeway, better comfort, and less wear on the boat and crew. The fact that we were so heavy and low in the water compounded the problem.

Lille Dansker had a lot of sheer that resulted in low freeboard amidships. The combination of low freeboard and a somewhat blunt bow with limited flare resulted in a wet boat. But we didn't know any better and came to believe that being constantly wet was just part of offshore sailing. To be fair, loading the boat too heavily and sailing too close to the wind were major factors. The bowsprit routinely touched the water, resulting in green water down the deck. Had we been more versed in proper loading and weight distribution and had we also cracked sheets a bit, we would have reduced the occurrence of boarding seas and would have sailed faster.

While we were able to balance the sails so that *Lille* self-steered for most of the voyage, there were plenty of times when steering by the compass was required. We found that "boxing the compass" (reciting the points of the compass in the correct order) made reading the compass easier, especially at night during the last hour of the trick at the helm when the watch-stander's mind started hallucinating and his eyes struggled to focus. At best, a sailboat in a seaway approximates a compass heading and tends to wander back and forth to either side of the desired compass heading. Therefore, steering to a point on the compass was significantly easier than trying to read the numbers to maintain a degree heading.

Lille's compass was set up with points and degrees; the points were 11.25 degrees apart and easier to read. They are noted as cardinal points, inter-cardinal points, half points, and quarter (by) points. We each became proficient at naming the 32 points of the compass clockwise and counterclockwise (north, north by east, north northeast, northeast by north, northeast, northeast by east, east northeast, east by north, east, and so on around the compass).We found it was useful to sing out relative bearings (relative to *Lille*'s bow) in the old style when directing the helmsman's eyes to something on the water (an object, an island, another vessel,

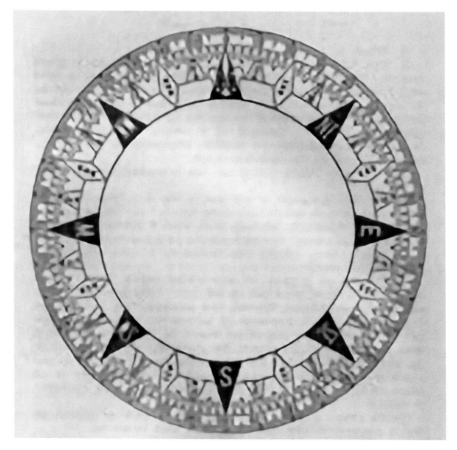

Boxing the compass

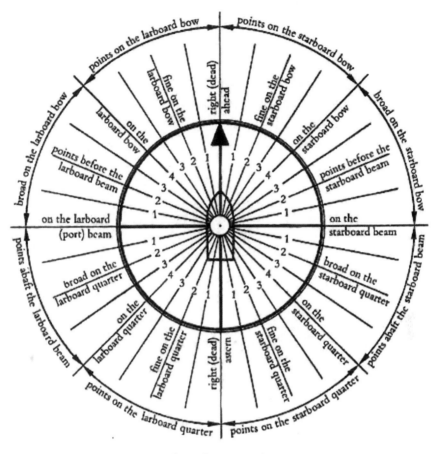

Relative bearing points

etc.). We were on a salty little ship, and the old lingo that had been around for hundreds of years still worked. Therefore, we learned to define the relative bearings by increments of compass points. For example, we would sing out "School of fish 2 points on the starboard bow." We also learned to say that same relative bearing as "fine on the starboard bow." Both expressions meant that the school of fish was approximately 22½ degrees to starboard of *Lille*'s bow. That method was intuitive once we got the hang of it.

As we eased down the track to Somewhere South, we came to realize that we had done a good job of preparing *Lille* for the voyage. We were well stocked with supplies, spares, maintenance gear, an extensive sail repair kit, emergency gear, and fishing gear. *Lille*'s hull and deck were sound, her sails were excellent, and even though we had occasional minor rigging issues, we felt confident that our vessel was in good shape and up to an extended voyage.

Perhaps we should have prepared ourselves better for the rigors of bluewater sailing. We were not adequately prepared for the frequent boarding seas. Clothing for each of us consisted mostly of a few swimsuits and T-shirts. We each brought a decent sweater and a pair of rubber boots. For nights in town, we each had one decent pair of shorts and one button-up shirt. I had an old pair of Topsiders for shore visits. John had wisely decided to splurge and purchase some quality foulweather gear. I went with a cheap rubberized set of raingear, and bought a sou'wester, since my foulies did not have an attached hood. Marc was a hardhead and bought a plastic poncho that was constantly flapping in the wind, so he rigged an elaborate web of small stuff to reef down the poncho. It didn't take long for me to realize that John had made a really good decision. But even with his quality foulies, John also suffered from the drenchings.

We were all constantly wet and developed sea boils on our butts. We were also constantly cutting our hands, and the cuts developed into salt-encrusted sea sores. Those little buggers were surprisingly painful and an incredible nuisance.

Catching fish was an especially critical component of our diet, and we were well prepared with fishing gear. John and I had been fishermen since childhood and were confident that with the right gear, we could keep the boat supplied with fish. Most of our fishing had been trolling in nearshore waters in the Gulf of Mexico. Bluewater fishing was new to us, but we figured trolling is trolling.

During the months prior to departure, we had been to the home of John Cobb-Adams a couple of times each week for dinner and conversation. Uncle Odie, as he preferred to be called, was a Honolulu Police Department Detective and a true Hawaiian gentleman. He was the real uncle of Rhoda Lum, John's girl-friend. Our discussions with Uncle Odie mostly involved the wonders of Hawaiian, Tahitian, Haole women and women in general, with occasional forays into fishing methods, sailing, skin-diving, and the ocean in general. Odie always got very emotional, his voice would fade, and his eyes would mist over as he tried to talk about the ocean. He held a deep, abiding love for the ocean and took great interest in our voyaging plans.

At the final dinner at his house prior to our departure, he gave us a splendid old Penn Senator 14-0 reel and a bag full of lures, and through sobs and tears managed to tell us that his fishing days were past, and he needed to know that his gift would help us on our way to the South Pacific. His gifts were our most prized possessions

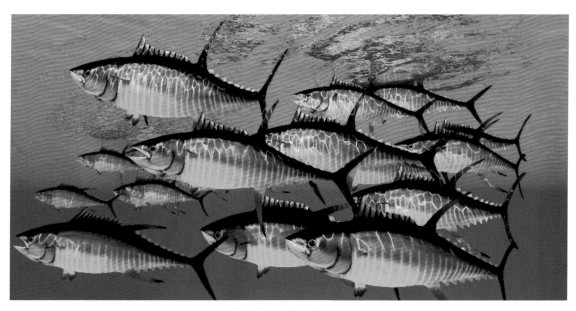

School of yellowfin tuna

on the boat. I know that I said a silent prayer for Odie each time I put a line out and each time we reeled in a fish, and I suspect that John did the same. We mounted the reel to a stern stanchion and set the drag very loose because we didn't have a fishing pole. Rigging a loop of line to the starboard aft mizzen shroud, attached with a rubber band, provided slack as soon as a fish hit the lure, and that helped. John was very keen on fishing, and there was seldom a time during daylight when there wasn't a lure in the water.

We soon learned that we did not want to catch big fish. We didn't have refrigeration, and a smallish, say 15-pound, fish would provide at least two meals for the three of us. But most of the lures in Uncle Odie's bag were large, intended for catching big ahi (yellowfin tuna) and those lures had large single or double hooks. We replaced the skirts and the large hooks for smaller hooks on some of the lures, and that worked, sort of. We still occasionally hooked a marlin or big ahi and almost immediately lost the whole shebang, including the lure, leader, and a lot of line or had to reel in as much line as possible and then try to shake the hook. We had to cut the line on one occasion.

Catching a large fish was irresponsible and could also cause some real damage to the cockpit and ourselves. We learned that early on the hard way by boating a large and very lively ahi before he or she was exhausted by the fight. That was an impressive sight. The ahi regurgitated a huge volume of recently swallowed smaller fish and squid, and there was blood everywhere. But the incredible thing was the power of that fish. Marc was quick to recognize that we had a real problem on our hands, in that the thrashing fish was about to splinter the lovely mahogany compass binnacle. Marc grabbed a wet towel to blanket the fish and he then stood on it. We all just had to sit down in awe, our faces and bodies splattered with blood and regurgitated fish guts, and our hearts racing. So cool, but once was enough.

We made some sashimi that evening, cooked up a feast that night, and then had a huge breakfast of ahi and scrambled eggs the next morning. We tried making fish jerky by cutting the remaining fish into thin slices and then hanging those slices on the lifelines to dry, but that didn't work. We were taking on waves that kept the strips wet, so we ended up throwing the slices back into the ocean.

Ahi tuna (*Thunnus albacares*) are found in tropical and subtropical pelagic waters. *Ahi* is a Hawaiian word meaning "fire" and comes from the smoke that a fishing line makes when the hooked fish dives and drags the fishing line over the gunwale of a fisherman's canoe.

These fish have attained near evolutionary perfection. They are "super fish," weighing up to 400 pounds, able to attain swimming speeds approaching 50 mph and dive to 3,000 feet deep. Tuna are the only endothermic (warm-blooded) fish, and that is what gives them advantage over other fishes. Their network of blood vessels keeps their muscles and organs warmer than the surrounding seawater, making tuna more efficient than their prey.

What I find most amazing about the ahi is the incredible hydrodynamic perfection of the fish's body. They are absolutely built for speed. The long pectoral fins are wings that generate lift but can be folded into perfectly faired depressions in the body when high speed is needed. The same is true for the first dorsal fin, leaving the scimitar-shaped second dorsal fin, anal fin, and small finlets to make minor course corrections during high-speed pursuit of prey. Every time we brought an ahi aboard, I took a few minutes to marvel at the evolutionary beauty of the animal.

We found that an easy and tasty method for cooking fish was to place slices of onion in the bottom of a deep pot, cover the onions with water and a touch of canned sweet milk, place fish fillets on the onions, put the lid on the pot, and then steam the fish. That did not require a lot of water or cleanup and cooked the fish in just a few minutes.

Cooking time was important because our stove was a very temperamental kerosene-burning affair that required lots of obsequious persuasion, prayers, and routine overhaul. John tried singing the stove's favorite Beatles tunes. Marc told dirty jokes to the stove. I read Robert Service poetry to the stove. None of that worked. The stove had the gall to laugh at us one evening when we were preparing to cook dinner, but the laughing stopped when Marc announced that he was going to cast it overboard.

The stove's kerosene tank was in the engineroom and had an air pump to pressurize the system. We had to preheat the burners by burning alcohol in the burner bowl and then pray that the kerosene would vaporize and ignite. More often than not it would flare up and coat the galley overhead with black smudge. We learned that keeping the burner jets clean and occasionally cleaning the kerosene tank were key to proper function.

We knew that we had a good boat when we started out on the voyage but came to realize that *Lille* was exceptionally comfortable down below. At night we routinely kept the kerosene lantern burning in the main saloon. The result was a cozy retreat for wet and cold watchstanders.

Lille on a reach

5

Daily Life

*L*ILLE DANSKER WAS A COZY BOAT with an interesting interior layout. She had a sizable chain locker with a watertight bulkhead separating it from the main saloon. The saloon side of the bulkhead had built-in drawers and bookshelves painted gloss white and trimmed with black walnut, giving the saloon a library-like feel. The mainmast was stepped just aft of the bulkhead and a folding table was aft of the mast. Settees were positioned on port and starboard. The backrest of each settee could be hinged down to provide a berth above and outboard of it. A cabinet of four drawers with a smallish, fiddled top was built in just aft of the port settee. We kept the radio direction finder (RDF) secured to the cabinet top. The hanging locker was just aft of the four-drawer cabinet.

When I purchased the boat, there was a wood-burning stove just forward of the galley on the port side. We tried to salvage the stove, but it was too far gone with rust. The galley was to port and at the base of the companionway.

The cooking stove was for some strange reason oriented athwartships and gim-balled fore and aft. That was a constant problem. Keeping pots stable when the boat heeled was a challenge, and there were several instances of dinner taking flight into the saloon. One instance comes to mind. We had been in strong winds for several days and everything was wet inside the cabin, which had taken on a sort of locker room/rancid clothes/mildewed-something essence. We had not been in dry clothes for days, and our bunks were wet and moldy. If this were to continue it might start to get a bit unpleasant, but we gathered in the main saloon and closed the compan-ionway hatch in preparation for a good, hearty meal.

It was John's turn to cook, and he was making a noble effort to produce some-thing hot and tasty for dinner. Well, at least hot. We hadn't had a hot meal in a few days due to the weather and the ongoing warfare with the cantankerous stove. John had mixed up a batch of something he called *lobscouse*, a mélange of beans, rice, potatoes, and a few other unmentionable canned selections in the large frying pan. He had somehow coerced the stove to cooperate. I don't remember precisely, but there may have been a few sardines in the mix or as a side dish.

We were ready to serve up the feast when the boat suddenly lurched to starboard and launched the fully loaded frying pan, which somehow miraculously landed flat on the cabin sole without spilling much of the lobscouse. John attempted to grab the pan, but the boat lurched back to port, causing John to stumble and plant his rubber-booted right foot square in the pan. As the boat made another heel to starboard John stumbled again, and we took note that his boot was wedged in the pan and then John and his boot lifted the pan off the cabin sole and the pan's contents were ejected onto the bulkheads, overhead, and occupants. We managed to salvage most of the meal, using gravity to recover the lobscouse from the overhead. John pried the pan off his boot, and we all set down to enjoy dinner.

After a few bites, John said, "Well, at least there's one good thing about it."

Marc and I waited to hear the one good thing. We waited some more. Finally, losing patience, Marc asked, "So what the hell is so good about this shitstorm?"

After another lengthy delay, John answered, "I'm thinking about it."

Other than the orientation of the cookstove, the galley was traditional for boats of that vintage. There was an icebox. Of course, we had no ice, so we used that space for more canned food storage. There was a single copper sink, and fresh water was supplied by a lovely old bronze lever-action hand pump. There were well-designed built-in cabinets and plate and flatware bins with fiddles.

Aft of the starboard settee was the beautifully crafted and functional nav station. It was also made of black walnut and had several slots and drawers for storing plotting tools and various odds and ends. A shelf beneath the nav desk was perfectly dimensioned for my Plath sextant box. I stored rolled charts in the overhead using bungee cord attached to the cabin trunk beams. We had a Yaesu ham radio on the shelf next to the sextant box. None of us had a ham license, so we only had the radio in case of dire emergency. We never made a call on that radio but did listen to the Pacific cruising net a couple of times. Frankly, I found the radio to be a nuisance and an intrusion into our otherwise independent and lonely adventure.

The head was located at the base of the companionway on the starboard side. It included a small porcelain sink with another smallish bronze lever-action hand pump. The head was a manual porcelain relic. Holding tanks were not part of the deal when the boat was built in 1947.

An oddity of the boat was that access to the 'midship cabin was through the head. It was just as well that we didn't use the head much anyway, choosing instead to hang over the stern. The rule was that he who clogged the head had to clean the

Squared away

head; therefore, being typical males, we totally avoided the problem by making the head off limits. Problem solved. As for after-action cleaning, we devised what we considered to be a very clever and simple method by tying a piece of cotton cloth to a stern stanchion with nylon paracord and dragging it in the wake. (Okay, granted that is disgusting and marginally sanitary, but it usually worked for us. Usually. Very early one morning, while on watch, I heard a commotion astern and looked back to see that a huge fish had chomped down on the cloth and the paracord had stretched out to twice its normal length. The fish suddenly released the cloth, which resulted in the cloth springing back at high speed and wrapping itself onto my face. That was an unusual and rather unpleasant way to start the day.)

John had the port-side bunk in the 'midships cabin and Marc had the starboard bunk. I bunked in the starboard-side fold-down berth in the main saloon. I wanted to be ready to bound out of the cabin if John or Marc called me during watches. There was a real fine built-in bookcase oriented athwartships between the 'midships cabin bunks and a 2-by-4-foot opening hatch in a trunk through the overhead of the cabin. The hatch itself was teak and had two round fixed portlights, and the trunk provided standing room. Access to the engine room was via an oval hatchway next to the bookcase.

The engine room was a spacious and well-organized wonder. The original power-plant installation included a Palmer 30-horsepower gas engine and a 12-volt U.S. Lighting plant. Both had been removed at some point and replaced with an Isuzu four-cylinder 50-horsepower diesel driving a three-bladed fixed pitch prop. The engine room allowed full crawl-around access to the engine and transmission. Batteries were stored in compartments built into the bulkhead. Storage bins were positioned port and starboard. The engine was a truck engine that had been marinized with a freshwater heat exchanger with seawater cooling provided by a belt-driven Jabsco pump. We also had a manual clutch-engaged, belt-driven Jabsco bilge pump that was a quality piece of gear. A hinged hatch opened from the engine room out into the cockpit doghouse.

The doghouse was the best feature of the boat. It had a rounded mahogany dodger, a reading light, and a cushioned seat. That combination kept the watch-stander reasonably dry and comfortable. Since *Lille* steered herself for most of the trip, provided we had the sails trimmed properly, most watch-standing was done from the confines of the doghouse, with routine exits for a 360 scan and for occasional gear and rigging inspections.

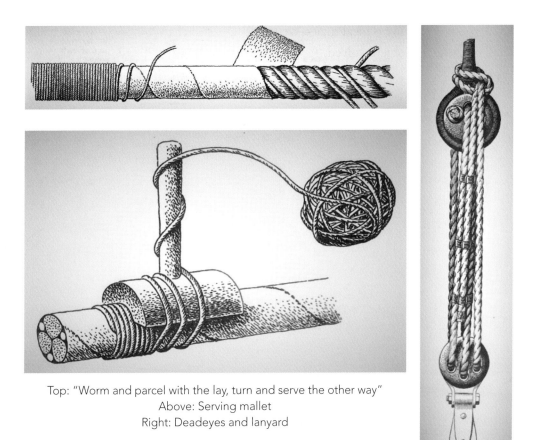

Top: "Worm and parcel with the lay, turn and serve the other way"
Above: Serving mallet
Right: Deadeyes and lanyard

Working sails included a clubfooted jib that tacked to the end of the bowsprit, a gaff-headed main, and a gaff-headed mizzen. The jib had two reefpoints. The main had three reefpoints, and the mizzen had two. The gaffs attached to the masts with saddles that had leather chafe protection where the saddle contacted the mast and a string of lignum vitae parrel balls surrounding the mast. The masts also had aluminum bands at the full-hoist, single-reef, and double-reef heights secured around the masts to prevent wear by the constant movement of the gaff saddles. Half-inch Dacron luff lacing started at the gaff saddle and was laced around the mast down to the gooseneck fitting. We also carried a 135 percent genoa, a main topsail, and a jib topsail. The mainmast and mizzenmast had running backstays. A triatic stay ran between the main topmast and the truck of the mizzenmast.

Shrouds were tensioned with lanyards rove through deadeyes. The main and

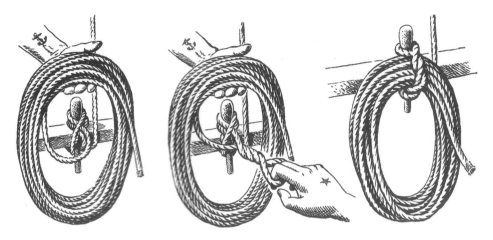

Coiling a halyard on a belaying pin

mizzen each had four-part blocks on both the peak and throat halyards. One man could easily hoist the sails. Emergency reefing was a matter of dropping the peak halyard to "scandalize" the sail, which reduced the sail area by about 50 percent. Teak belaying-pin bars were secured between the lower shrouds port and starboard on the main and mizzen. We coiled and stowed the halyards on the starboard belaying pins. Ratlines were lashed between the port and starboard shrouds on the main and mizzen. We purchased a new jib, main, and mizzen for the voyage.

The original shrouds were galvanized wire rope and were spliced to deadeyes and tensioned with tarred right-laid three-strand Italian hemp lanyards at the lower ends. There were no turnbuckles integrated with the shrouds. The wire was treated in accordance with the old saying, "Worm and parcel with the lay, turn and serve the other way." When preparing for the voyage we kept the deadeyes but changed the tired shrouds to 7-by-19 stainless steel and used three-strand Dacron for the lanyards. I like preserving old stuff, but I am not a purist when it comes to practicality. The lanyards were reeved through the upper deadeye starting with a Matthew Walker knot and then multi-parted through the lower deadeyes.

Tuning each shroud was a simple matter of tensioning a multi-part lanyard by laying back on the running parts one by one until attaining proper tension and then securing the bitter end with a cow hitch. For rigging instruction we relied on sketches of deadeyes and lanyards, a serving mallet, and the process of worming and parceling found in Hervey Garret Smith's marvelous book, *The Marlinspike Sailor*.

Our ship's library included that book and his other excellent reference book, *The Arts of the Sailor*.

We made a crude but workable serving mallet and replaced the bobstay by "worming, parceling, turning, and serving" a bit of the old, galvanized wire rope. Full disclosure—we didn't eyesplice the ends of the new bobstay, opting for simpler Nicopress sleeves. We eventually got competent at splicing wire rope when we had to replace a running backstay. We also ran the bobstay through a length of PVC pipe to prevent anchor rode chafing.

We wore out most pages of both of Hervey's books as we practiced making knots, bends, and fancy rope work while on watch. When one of us asked how some rigging repair should proceed, the answer was always, "Ask Hervey." Every proper cruising boat library should include both of Mr. Smith's excellent books.

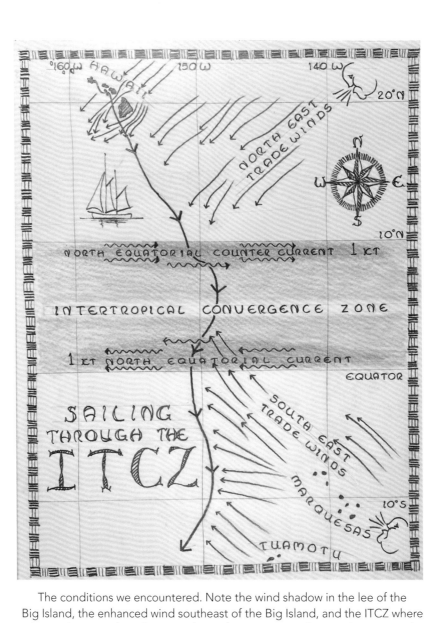

The conditions we encountered. Note the wind shadow in the lee of the Big Island, the enhanced wind southeast of the Big Island, and the ITCZ where the northeast and southeast trade winds converge at about 6 degrees north latitude. The arrowed line approximates our 1977 track through the area.

6

Intertropical Convergence Zone

JULY 17 STARTED ROUTINELY with our regular breakfast of grapefruit and granola with wheat germ and plastic milk. Our noon position had us in 10 degrees 30 minutes north, 150 degrees 15 minutes west, which put us 180 nautical miles west of our departure planning waypoint. We obviously were not going to make that waypoint, but we were starting to figure out that maintaining boat speed was important.

The trade winds backed to north-northeast and maintained 15 to 20 knots for much of the day, providing us with a wonderful reach easing down 8–10-foot seas. *Lille* was in heaven. John caught a nice mahi mahi, and we had a particularly good dinner.

We always tried to finish dinner and wash dishes before sunset so that we had time to settle the boat in for the night watches. And, we found it comforting to gather in the cockpit at sunset. Having time to reflect on the day and converse about anything that came to mind was an effective way to ease the nervousness that darkness might bring.

When planning the voyage, we had thought that we would want to share a beer or have a shot of brandy or rum each evening, but found that just relaxing and talking was better. I developed a genuine appreciation for night watches and learned to cherish time in the cockpit with the stars and ocean. Seems to me that boats also enjoy nighttime sailing; they seem to settle down a bit.

That evening we stayed in the cockpit longer than normal and Marc, who was normally quiet and reticent, opened up about some of his experiences as a UDT diver, when he had experienced some tough situations. I hit the rack about 2200.

Marc called for me at midnight. Coming on deck I found that the wind had dropped to nothing, but we still had a trade wind swell. Marc was dropping the main and mizzen to stop the slatting sails and banging gaffs. We hoped the wind would come back soon, but we wallowed for the remainder of the night and well into the next morning, at which point we realized that we had probably arrived in the Intertropical Convergence Zone (ITCZ). Perhaps I should refer to it as *Zone de Convergence Intertropicale* since we were headed towards French Polynesia.

We were surprised at how suddenly we had transitioned from perfect wind conditions to nothing. It was as if Mother Ocean was just giving us a gentle nudge into the ITCZ so that the momentum might carry us across to the southeast trades. However, the swell gradually diminished, and we were left parked in a void. That was a good thing as it gave us a chance to dry out the boat. We opened all the hatches, and brought clothes, linens, and mattresses on deck to air out in the bright sun.

We swam a couple of times during the afternoon. We checked the bottom and prop; both were fairly clean. A big ahi that had been trailing us for a few days approached a few times, always on the port quarter.

Marc went aloft to install a newly spliced port main running backstay. I repaired one of the mizzen sheet blocks and replaced two broken piston hanks on the jib. John renewed the leather in the galley freshwater pump, then we all tackled the kerosene tank and stove burners again.

We had an excellent dinner of canned Dinty Moore beef stew with the last of our fresh carrots, potatoes, and onions thrown in. The highlight of the meal was freshly baked Bisquick biscuits topped off with homemade mixed-fruit jam that had been given to us by a voluptuous female friend on departure day. We referred to the jam as Melon Jam: "Please pass the Melon Jam." "I'll have another serving of that luscious Melon Jam."

Given the calm conditions, we decided that we all needed a good sleep, so we got *Lille* put to bed and hit the rack ourselves. That didn't last long. Around midnight I went topside to check on things to find John making rigging checks up forward. Then Marc came up to do the same. We had become programmed by then to constant attention to *Lille*'s well-being.

We decided to hang out in the cockpit for another conversation and brought the radio direction finder on deck to try to find some music on the AM band. We didn't have any other kind of sound system, and the sound from the RDF speaker was a bit tinny, but that was okay. We were able to tune into KPOI AM 830 out of Honolulu and listened to a brief bit of Hawaii news and some good music. We lost reception as the sun appeared.

By late morning we had the boat dried out and squared away, went for a quick swim, and then fired up the engine and started motoring southeast. While we wanted to cross the ITCZ in the most direct route (due south), we also wanted to take advantage of the eastward-flowing North Equatorial Counter-Current (NECC) in hopes of gaining some much-needed easting.

Nature does not abide imbalance, and the convergence of the two trade wind systems results in a state of near constant imbalance, with nature struggling to make things right. She can get a bit testy with the chaos and create considerable unwanted drama for sailors. The ITCZ is a strange and bewildering area of wildly variable weather conditions, including dead calms, spectacular cloud bursts, and sudden and ferocious squalls.

Sailors commonly refer to the ITCZ as the doldrums in reference to the mind-anesthetizing calms. However, most Shellbacks (those who have previously sailed across the equator and have been initiated into the Order of Neptune) have endured nasty weather before and after experiencing doldrums as they worked their way through the ITCZ. This area encircles the Earth near the thermal equator and its position varies seasonally. In the Central Pacific during July and August, the ITCZ normally occurs within a band of latitude between 2 and 10 north, but it can also occur south of the equator.

Due to the Coriolis effect, which is imparted by the Earth's rotation, the southeast trades are forced around to the southwest where the wind crosses the equator, thus opposing the northeast trades and creating an area of low pressure. In this case the system is also referred to as the Near-Equatorial Trough. The Coriolis effect also causes the NECC, which only occurs when the ITCZ is north of the equator. In addition to the trough at the equator, a ridge forms at about 5 degrees north and another trough forms at about 10 degrees north, with the NECC normally located in between. Many sailors have been fooled into thinking that after passing through one of the troughs and then into the clear skies of the ridge, and even though still in light air, they have made it out of the ITCZ, only to then pass back into the next trough with more boredom and/or excitement.

We motored until mid-morning the next day when an engine check revealed that the belt-driven raw water pump was cracked and spraying water all over the engine room. We shut down, removed the water pump, and discussed a repair method. The housing was cracked, and we devised a plan to encase the housing with fiberglass, using materials from our surfboard repair kit. We had neglected to bring a spare water pump; our spares inventory was well stocked otherwise. Marc went to work on the pump while John and I raised full sail to nurse *Lille* out of the void. There was just no wind, so we doused the sails. The environment was absolutely quiet, something that I had never experienced. No sound of any kind.

My noon celestial fix that day put us in 8 degrees 55 minutes north, 149 degrees 20 minutes west, and confirmed that we were indeed in the NECC and were being carried due east by the approximate 1-knot current. We started feeling a very light east-southeast breeze that evening, hoisted full sail, and started moving. Marc's water-pump repair job went through a few iterations as we slowly worked *Lille* due south. We had to sheet the sails right in to keep them from slatting in the light air, so the sails were not breathing, and we were not sailing efficiently but at least we were moving in the right direction.

We also rigged a spare mizzen halyard from the top of the mizzenmast to the peak of the main gaff as a gaff preventer. That managed to calm down the main gaff but presented a problem when a sudden rain squall caught us unaware. The normal procedure in a squall was to scandalize the main by dropping the peak halyard and then drop the throat halyard if the squall had some ass in it. We had forgotten about the gaff preventer and got all fouled up. Fortunately, the squall didn't have much ass, and we got squared away and put a reef in the main.

The good thing about rain squalls in the ITCZ is that they can dump a lot of water in very short order. We came up with a way to catch rainwater in the folds of the reefed main by attaching a bucket to the end of the boom and slacking the peak halyard to drop the boom a bit, so that the captured water ran into the bucket. There is nothing tastier than cool rainwater, and we managed to top up our water tanks with delicious, sweet rainwater while in the ITCZ. *Lille's* water tanks were bronze, and if we kept the tanks clean with occasional doses of baking soda, the water always had a pleasant taste. Filling the tanks was a real confidence boost since we had been very conscious of water consumption.

After four days of the light air, we managed to sail 178 miles due south and found ourselves in 6 degrees north, 149 degrees west, where the winds shut down all together. While we had only averaged 44.5 nautical miles per day, at least we had been moving. During those four days we read some good books, practiced marline-spike seamanship under Hervey's tutelage, and generally enjoyed being in that very strange environment as we moseyed along towards Somewhere South.

We made and rigged new baggywrinkle for the mainmast after shrouds, which protected the mainsail from chafe. We had purchased a spool of old ½-inch manila

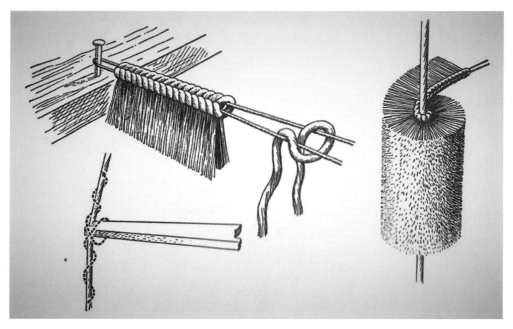

Making baggywrinkle

line at a marine auction and used that to make the baggywrinkle. We also "rattled down the shrouds," which is an old square-rigger term for installing ratlines. Ratlines are either rope or wooden steps rigged horizontally between shrouds to provide a ladder for going aloft. Our ratlines were wooden.

One day Marc spotted a gray plastic jug just off the port bow, and we picked it up. It was about 20-gallon capacity with Italian embossing. The outside was very clean, and the cap was screwed down tight. We opened the jug to find that it contained a few cups of red wine. We shared a cup of the wine that night at dinner and were delighted to discover that it provided a focused and woody symphony of flavors with just a hint of almond and… Okay, the wine was awful and came from a 20-gallon plastic jug that had likely been thrown overboard from a nasty old tramp steamer. But for us the wine was magnificent.

During the next rain squall, we decided to fill the jug without rinsing it first. We occasionally shared a mug of wine-imbued rainwater after dinner and toasted the ship that had provided the gift. We decided that the ship was an Italian freighter captained by a tyrannical feckless drunk. Picture Benito Mussolini with an eye patch and a peg leg. Why not, right?

Marc had completed the water-pump repair and we decided to give it a test run.

We got underway and while the pump leaked some, we had good water flow from the exhaust. But we could only make about 3 knots. We shut down, looked over the engine, and considered that we might have picked up a net or other debris on the prop or shaft. John donned his mask and dove in, returning almost immediately to say, "You might want to take a look at this."

Marc and I put on masks and jumped in to find that the entire bottom of the boat was carpeted with goose barnacles, thousands and thousands, each about an inch long. How had that happened in only a few days, and where had they come from? We discussed it and assumed that we must have drifted through a massive bloom of homeless barnacle larvae ready to take occupancy.

Continuing to motor with a fouled bottom would have just wasted fuel, so we got started scraping the bottom with various tools and soon learned that cleaning the bottom of a boat in even a slight swell is dangerous, as the boat heaves up and down and the likelihood of banging our heads was a problem. We solved that by strapping tight lines around the hull to provide a handhold to maintain our vertical position relative to the hull.

As we scraped off the goose barnacles, they fell away in a cloud of delicious tidbits that attracted schools of small fish that appeared out of nowhere. That was very strange. Where had they been before and how did they know that we were preparing lunch for them? And of course, bigger fish soon followed, and we had our friendly ahi and several large mahi mahi rampaging through the cloud and feasting on the small fish that were feasting on the barnacles.

I looked up to see that Marc had climbed aboard and retrieved his speargun. He missed a couple of times but then nailed a nice mahi mahi of about 15 pounds. It was a gut shot and the fish fought for a few seconds before Marc could gather in the tether and hand the fish up to John. There were a few dark shapes appearing down deep, so we hurried to finish cleaning the hull—and then all the sea life just disappeared as if nothing had happened. It made me wonder where all our pelagic friends hung out regularly. There must certainly be some sophisticated form of communication amongst fishes to inform others that a food source is in the offing.

We baked the mahi mahi for dinner. John had heard or read somewhere that goose barnacles make for a good soup base, and he had gathered and kept about two cups full of the barnacles while cleaning the hull. We cooked the barnacles in water seasoned with Zatarain's Crab Boil. I can say with conviction that the mahi mahi was excellent.

We decided we should limit use of the engine to save the questionable water pump for our eventual arrival somewhere. We also discussed a backup plan for the water pump. We figured that we could put our spare electric submersible bilge pump in a 5-gallon bucket, disconnect the engine driven pump from the raw-water intake hose, lash that hose into the bucket, and then plumb the bilge pump exhaust into the engine seawater intake. We tried it and it worked just fine.

So, we had a backup but still thought it prudent to sail our way out of the void. So, we hoisted sail yet again and nursed *Lille* along. We even hoisted the main top-sail and the jib topsail. Wish we could have gotten some photos, since that was the only time we sailed with that fully rigged configuration.

Fortunately, the barnacles did not repopulate *Lille*'s bottom. That reinforced our theory that we had drifted through a larvae bloom.

Oceanic blue shark

7

White Squall
and Blue Sharks

W E DOUSED THE MAIN TOPSAIL and the jib topsail for the night watches and continued in light airs with full working sails. I was on watch at about 0430 the next morning when I felt a sudden blast of cold air. I jumped up and looked to weather to see a huge white mass barreling down on us. I called down for all hands, let the mizzen halyards run, scandalized the main, and had made my way forward to pull down the jib when we got knocked down and pinned to the water. John, on deck by then, helped me to fully douse the main and recover the jib, which would have been shredded had we not got it down soon.

Briefly closing my eyes, I pictured a freight train plowing right over us. The sound of the wind was magnificent and deafening. *Lille* was lying on her starboard side and we were just managing to hang on as she slowly righted herself. Marc had also climbed and clawed his way topside and took the helm to turn *Lille* into the wind.

Getting knocked down can be a real problem if something carries away or the boat is swamped. In our case, *Lille* was not swamped and nothing broke, but it certainly got our attention. It was a close call, that. An overly simplified formula to compute wind force on an object is:

F (wind force in pounds per square foot) = 0.004 x V (wind velocity in miles per hour) squared

The vital point is that the force is the square of the wind speed, and forces change very rapidly in a squall. Assuming that before the squall hit we had been sailing on a beam reach in a wind of 10 miles per hour with full sails, the force on the boat would have been about 500 pounds. With full sails in a 60-mile-per-hour squall, the initial force on the boat would have been about 13,000 pounds and we would have blown out sails or worse. That is why getting sails down immediately is key. Our saving grace was that as the boat heeled to leeward, the exposed surface

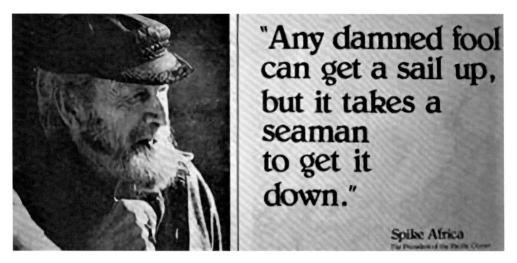

"Any damned fool can get a sail up, but it takes a seaman to get it down."

Spike Africa
The President of the Pacific Ocean

Spike Africa, first mate aboard schooner *Wanderer* and president of the Pacific Ocean

area was reduced, since the sails were no longer perpendicular to the wind. Therefore, the wind force dropped, Marc upped the helm, and the weight of the lead keel overcame the wind force and righted the boat. Turning into the wind also significantly reduced the exposed surface area.

I paused to consider that we had developed into a finely tuned crew. While we still had a lot to learn about sailing and sometimes our inexperience got us into questionable situations, we were working well together and having one hell of a grand adventure. I mean, getting knocked down in a white squall was excellent fun once we realized that *Lille* was okay. The wind was ferocious. I have no idea of the wind speed, but the sea was blown flat and there was a solid layer of *ehu kai* (sea spray) up at least to the top of the mainmast. Marc's plastic poncho was blown to bits that skipped over the sea downwind. My sou'wester suffered the same fate. So AWESOME!

It was hard to come down from that kind of high, but I busied myself squaring away the sails and rigging and then just looked out at the ocean and gave thanks for the experience.

I can only assume that we had encountered a white squall caused by a dry microburst. The winds only lasted a few minutes and there was no rain associated with the initial wind blast. We had already experienced several rain squalls as we made our way through the ITCZ, but the winds of a rain squall are accompanied by black clouds and a sudden downpour.

Typically, rain squalls are followed by a period of very light wind, a sort of vacuum on the back side of the squall. That situation was initially very frustrating as we had to fight our way out of the squall only to find ourselves becalmed with slatting sails for an extended period as Mother slowly got things squared away and balanced. That is just one more aspect of the chess game known as the ITCZ that drives sailors to distraction. I soon learned to think of the ITCZ as a challenging science project and was then able to marvel at the diversity, wonder of the ocean, and weather conditions we encountered.

We changed the watch schedule to maintain a two-man watch until we were truly back into more predictable trade wind conditions. One man was always alert, and the other was allowed to sleep in the doghouse, but ready to jump if a squall popped up.

We were committed to somehow working our way out of the nothingness. But, there was no wind and the air was thick and bloody hot. Since we were obviously not going to be doing any meaningful sailing, we took advantage of the situation to go for a swim and check *Lille*'s bottom again. I put on a mask, snorkel, and fins and dove in.

The water was as clear as air, making it appear that I might easily fall into the abyss, causing me to instinctively reach for *Lille*'s support. Realizing that I wasn't going to fall, I swam down to about 40 feet and rolled onto my back to look up at *Lille*. She looked peaceful and happy. Then, looking back down into the blue, I noticed two shapes emerging from the deep. The shapes became two gorgeous oceanic blue sharks, gracefully meandering back and forth as they slowly ascended towards me. Right then, I knew that we were amid something incredibly import-ant, not knowing what that really meant, but certain that we were inconsequential participants in something very profound.

I slowly kicked to the surface. Marc and John were preparing to dive overboard. I told them that two blue sharks were making their way to the boat. Marc immedi-ately dove in and swam down. I watched him descend. Hard to know how deep he went because the clarity and magnifying effect of the water made depth perception difficult. Marc stopped for what seemed like minutes. John had entered the water by then and we swam partway down to meet Marc, who signaled that he was com-ing up. When we had all reached the surface, I suggested that we get back on the boat, so John and I climbed aboard but Marc stayed in the water off the starboard side amidships.

Marc in companionway

The blue sharks surfaced about 20 feet from the boat. They appeared to be about 10 feet long, which is typical of adult female oceanic blues. John and I leaned over the rail preparing to lift Marc aboard. One of the sharks swam slowly towards Marc. Marc kept his head submerged watching the approaching shark, and the shark gently bumped her snout against Marc's face plate. She turned and slowly swam away, sweeping her beautiful tail against Marc, who then climbed aboard and removed his mask, exclaiming, "Man, that was the coolest thing ever." Like I said, the guy was fearless. We didn't know if the sharks were aggressive or simply curious, but Marc just had to be in there with the sharks and was very humble in his fearlessness as if going nose to nose with a 10-foot shark was an everyday occurrence.

We jumped back in and watched the oceanic blues circle the boat in a gradually increasing radius, indicating that they no longer found us interesting. A few more blues appeared in the depths. It seemed strange but somehow comforting that they were there. We were 1,000 miles from nowhere and they were there for us.

During the following months in French Polynesia, we became somewhat comfortable swimming with sharks, because the options were to swim with them or stay out of the water, especially in the Tuamotu Archipelago. Here's a surefire way to test for sharks in the water. Taste the water—if it is salty, there are sharks in the water.

We swam a few more times to cool down that afternoon. A very light breeze came up and we made 1 to 2 knots due south during the night, experiencing only one squall.

Lille Dansker sailing "full and by"

8

Crossing the Line

Early the next morning, before going off watch I leaned over the stern and speared a pompano sort of fish using a Hawaiian sling (a three-prong spear with a surgical-tubing arbalete). The fish had been drafting us all night. We cooked it along with eggs and Bisquick pancakes for breakfast. Before we could sit down to enjoy breakfast, a squall bore down on us, so we had to reef, but we managed to catch 7 gallons of rainwater in various buckets. It worked out well because we were then in the vacuum on the backside of the squall and had calm conditions for breakfast in the main cabin. The fish was very tasty.

During the meal we heard a hissing noise coming from the bilge, and after removing a floorboard, found that a can of Rainier beer had sprung a leak and was expelling itself into the bilge. We had been planning to celebrate the equator crossing with a cool beer but discovered that most of the other cans had already exploded due to the occasional corrosive saltwater bath in the bilge. We had to toss all the cans that had been stowed in the bilge…should have put them in John's bunk.

We sailed through a minor squall at 0200 on the morning of July 26 and by 0400 the wind was hinting at solid southeast trades. I was able to get a Venus line of position (LOP) at dawn, a sun line mid-morning, and another sun line in mid-afternoon. The wind held steady all day. Marc made a hearty dinner and we played poker until 2100. I had already learned that playing poker with John was a losing proposition, but since we were only betting with Saloon Pilot Crackers, I accepted the risk and forfeited my stash.

We sailed through a beautiful rain squall at sunrise the next morning. *Lille* was galloping along full and by in a flat sea while we took rainwater showers on deck using Dial bar soap and egg shampoo. That was a treat, because our normal seawater baths required using harsh dishwashing soap.

High cirrus clouds appeared that afternoon, and we noted the falling barometer. By evening the sky was 8/8 overcast and we were soon sailing in a steady rain.

The wind clocked to south-southeast on July 28, so we were not making a good course for Tahiti. The pilot chart for July showed a westerly flowing current of

1 knot at 2 degrees north, 150 degrees west, which exacerbated our problem. Fortunately, the skies cleared a bit, and I was able to get a fix shooting the upper limb of the moon and three stars just before dawn on the 29th. The moon was full the next day. The wind backed further to the east around noon.

Around sunset the headstay parted at the main topmast, so we rigged the genoa halyard as a stay. Making the repair in the current weather conditions was going to be a challenge. The wind later increased to 15–20 knots, and that negated any chance of going aloft. It would just have to wait, but our course was good, and we were making decent speed. As it turned out we were not able to complete the repair until we were safely anchored in calm conditions.

At 2238 GMT (Greenwich Mean Time) on July 31 we crossed the equator at 150 degrees 50 minutes west longitude. Marc had found a random can of beer in a storage locker while cleaning, and we shared that and made an offering to Mother Ocean during the transition into the South Pacific. John climbed to the crosstrees. I stood on my head with my feet braced against the doghouse. Marc chose to jump into the water and get dragged across the line, while sipping his share of the beer. There were no Shellbacks aboard to abuse us Pollywogs (first-time equator crossers), so we didn't make much of a ceremony of it. It was a big achievement for us, nonetheless. We learned there is not actually a line painted on the equator.

We also learned that flying fish making crash landings aboard during the night are tasty when deep-fried; rice cooked in seawater is not tasty.

Interestingly, the water and air temperatures were considerably cooler than just a couple of days before, meaning that we must have been getting some remnant effect of the Humboldt Current. The seawater bucket bath that afternoon was actually invigorating. The Humboldt Current runs up the west coast of South America bringing cold, low-salinity sub-Antarctic water, resulting in coastal water temperatures as low as 16°C (61°F) at 5 degrees south latitude. As the current turns west approaching the equator, becoming the South Equatorial Current, the water temperature gradually increases.

The Galápagos Islands, straddling the equator at 91 west longitude partially in the path of the Humboldt Current, have an average annual water temperature of 21°C (70°F). For comparison, the annual water temperature in Hawaii, which is located approximately 1,250 nautical miles north of the equator, is 25.5°C (78°F)—big difference. Our equator crossing position was approximately 3,600 nautical miles west

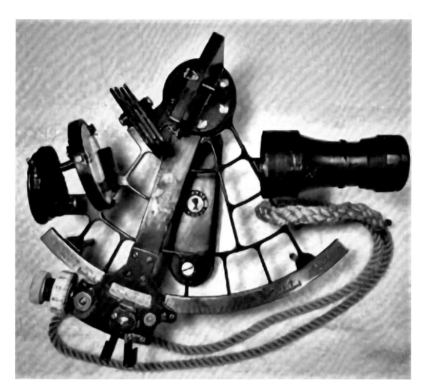

My Plath sextant

of the Galápagos, and I found it interesting that the water temperature remained cool for the approximate 150 days it took for the water to travel that distance.

Celestial navigation was one of the aspects of the voyage that I enjoyed most. Successful navigation can be challenging but can also be very gratifying if done well. I had purchased a 1957 vintage Plath sextant from a marine antiques dealer in Taiwan and only had to replace the mirrors. That sextant was my faithful companion throughout the voyage and for many subsequent voyages.

Ideally, I acquired a position fix each day if weather conditions allowed. In mid-ocean a fix that was accurate to within a mile or so was acceptable, but as the boat approached landfall, the navigation accuracy needed to improve. In mid-ocean I relied on a morning sun sight and an afternoon sun sight, advancing, and retarding the lines of position (LOP) to noon.

I had set up the watch schedule so that I was on watch at dawn and dusk to get star sights if needed. We generally stood four-hour watches unless we were hand-steering, in which case we reduced the trick to two hours. I soon realized how fortunate I was to have the privilege to witness every sunrise and sunset. Sunrises were especially pleasant, and it seemed to me that *Lille* felt the same. She just seemed to be relaxed and comfortable during that time of day. For morning sun sights, I waited until the sun was at least 20 degrees above the horizon to avoid refraction errors, took the sight, and then hit the rack. That worked fine, but occasionally, if we had a clear horizon at dawn or dusk, I took star sights. As we approached landfall, I took more frequent star, planet, and moon sights.

Later in the voyage when we were south of the equator, I managed to get a couple of local apparent noon (LAN) fixes, which worked well because the sun's declination was still in the northern hemisphere. LAN fixes are difficult when the vessel's latitude is close to the sun's declination.

At dawn on August 2, I was able to shoot Venus, Sirius, and the moon and plotted an accurate position. John had gone down with a stomach illness the day before. Marc and I shared the watches so that John could rest. He was back in business by August 4 in time for some glorious sailing and a magnificent night watch. The sky was crystal clear, the Southern Cross showed herself, and our wake was filled with bioluminescence caused by dinoflagellates, organisms in the surface layers of the ocean that illuminate when disturbed by a passing vessel. The bucket bath on deck that evening was perfect, with the bioluminescent water making our skin glow in the dark.

The water temperature was a little warmer than it had been near the equator. I brought the RDF on deck and managed to find a station playing a random mix of classical music. Somehow the music, the period of the swell, *Lille's* surges, and the pressure of the wind all jelled into perfect harmony as we soared along magically. Even the heavens seemed to be moving in time with the music. Night watches can be an absolute treasure.

The chart showed "Breakers (rep 1944)" off our starboard bow, so we sailed full and by and passed well to weather of the area, then cracked off a bit after passing.

At dawn on August 6 a pod of dolphins surrounded the boat, so I rigged a line from the samson post thru the starboard side hawsepipe, put a bowline in the end about amidships, donned a mask and snorkel, and went over the side. The wind was very light, and we were creeping along at about 1 knot, so I was able to pull myself up the knotted line to within a few feet of the bow. Gliding along with *Lille*, I was watching the dolphins lazily play on the bow wave, then peel off and circle back to come within arm's length of me. One youngster swam on his side and then belly-up, staying right beside me and maintaining steady eye contact. I reached out and he brushed my hand. Then they were suddenly all gone. I guess our slow speed didn't provide enough bow wave surfing. Sliding back, hand over hand, along the line to the waist of the boat and then diving down while still holding on, I noticed that we had several hitchhiking remoras, and our big ahi friend was still with us on the port quarter. We were becoming quite the big family.

When I climbed back onto the boat, John was upset. He had just come on deck and thought that I was gone. But when I explained about being with the dolphins, he calmed down. I acknowledged that it was supremely stupid of me and that if the opportunity presented itself again, any one of us desiring to take a dip would first alert someone before going over the side.

We passed 50 nautical miles east of Caroline Island on August 8, after a rough night of numerous squalls. John took the sun sights and did the computations, and the fix worked out perfectly. He sure picked up basic celestial navigation fast.

The three of us then took time to really study the charts and decided that perhaps we should head for Bora Bora, which was then 490 nautical miles at 197 degrees true. The place had a really cool name, and would be easier to lay than Papeete.

Sailing in Bora Bora lagoon

9

Landfall Bora Bora

OVER THE NEXT FEW DAYS, the southeast trade winds increased to a steady 25–30 knots and the seas got up to 12–15 feet. We sailed with deep reefs during the days and dropped the main at night. Gear started breaking as we pounded towards Bora Bora. That was okay because when something broke, we jumped right on it and just kept moving forward. *Lille* started complaining a bit, so we took it easy for the last 150 miles. The port forward mizzen chainplate broke, so we secured the shroud deadeye with Dacron line multi-parted through a deck scupper and that worked fine. Everything below got wet again. We were limping to the barn.

I managed to get a local apparent noon (LAN) fix, which worked well. I was also able to use the radio direction finder for an additional LOP. There was a good AM station in Papeete that we had first started receiving at night when we were about 700 miles out. That provided a good navigation check and was something that was available day and night once we got closer. That simple instrument provided reassurance along with some good Tahitian music. The accuracy of the RDF bearings improved as we got closer to Tahiti. As we approached the islands, I was not getting much sleep due to the heavy weather, rough seas, and the anticipation of making a landfall, so just having a quick and simple navigation check was comforting.

I was able to get a three-star fix at dawn on August 12. The weather was fine all morning with only random trade wind cumulus clouds. An early afternoon DR (dead reckoning) put us 25 nautical miles north of Bora Bora. I called up to Marc to go aloft and look forward for a green glow on the horizon. We had read somewhere that the turquoise color of the water of an atoll's lagoon can be reflected in the clouds above the lagoon. Sure enough, Marc yelled down that the glow was dead ahead. It was Tupai Atoll, about 15 miles north of Bora Bora. Then, almost immediately, Marc sang out "LAND HO, Bora Bora, fine on the port bow." He was seeing Mount Otemanu (2,385 feet), the highest peak on Bora Bora, in the background of the green glow. Too much! It was indeed a beautiful sight.

Landfalls are always a highlight of a voyage, and that one was a peach. The song

Bora Bora

"Bali Hai" from the movie *South Pacific* got stuck in my head: "Here am I, your special island. Come to me, come to me…"

Things were looking good for a daylight arrival, but when we sailed into the lee of Tupai Atoll the wind went light and remained light for the final 15 miles. We arrived at the entrance to Passe Teavanui, Bora Bora, at 1900 local time, too late to enter the channel. We had perfect light air and flat-water sailing conditions in the lee of Bora Bora, and spent the whole night cleaning and organizing the boat and listening to Radio Tahiti as we tacked back and forth offshore the channel.

We had each read Eric Hiscock's books by then and ascribed to his tenet that a boat should arrive looking better than she did at departure. While that is a bit unrealistic, we gave it our best effort and *Lille* was feeling damn good about herself.

The aromas drifting off the island were wonderful. That was a big surprise. We could actually smell dirt and plants. But the predominant aroma drifting from Bora Bora was the smell of burning coconut husks from the many cooking fires onshore. There was no way that we could sleep, so we just cleaned and organized and cleaned some more all night, while standing one-hour watches. The anticipation was incredible.

At dawn, using our spare bilge pump in the bucket system for engine cooling, we motor-sailed into the lagoon of the island that James Michener described as the most beautiful island in the world. Hard to argue with that—the beauty of the sunrise over the island was almost overwhelming.

We found Passe Teavanui wide and clearly marked through the reef, and after entering the lagoon we initially tried to make up to the village pier at Vaitape. Our intent was to clear customs, but we realized that the customs people might still be asleep, so we decided to relocate to Faanui Bay and then dropped anchor in about 13 fathoms among three other boats.

We hoisted the French flag and the solid yellow quarantine flag on the starboard spreader courtesy flag halyard. Marc and John unbagged and inflated the IBS (Inflatable Boat Small). Marc had acquired the IBS through the Navy surplus system. It was the type of boat that he and his Navy UDT buddies used regularly when conducting beach reconnaissance surveys. It served as our dinghy for the entire trip. We didn't have an outboard and the boat was difficult for one man to paddle, but it was extremely stable and rugged and came with a large upright manual air pump and four haze-gray paddles. We named it *Haze Gray and Underway*.

We paddled over to a handsome yacht named *Volunteer* and spoke with the owners Dave and Jane, who advised how to get to the customs office. We then paddled to shore and made up alongside the concrete dock. John climbed onto the dock and immediately lost his balance and fell. Marc and I had a good laugh until we climbed up and then also fell down. What the heck? The walk to the customs office in Vaitape village took up the entire road as we meandered back and forth, attempting to gain our land legs. Fortunately, in 1977 the coral perimeter road around Bora Bora was the only road and had essentially no traffic, so our winding route was not a problem. We provided some good entertainment for the residents, and we were to soon learn that Tahitians absolutely love to laugh. Several boys started mimicking our drunken walk, so of course we exaggerated the situation and fell occasionally. Good fun!!

Prior to leaving Honolulu we had purchased a paperback English-Tahitian dictionary and had tried to master a few expressions during the voyage. We had learned that *Ia ora na* is the Tahitian equivalent to the Hawaiian *Aloha,* so we figured that was the one word that we should get right. Good idea, except that our Southern-accented atrocious pronunciation resulted in something that confounded anyone with whom we spoke.

We stopped at a roadside grass-shack fruit stand and gave the elderly lady proprietor some American coins in exchange for a hand of bananas and three green drinking coconuts. Very refreshing! I attempted to say *Mauruuru roa* (thank you very much) and thought that I had done an admirable job. She patiently and politely responded in English: "I appreciate your efforts to speak our language, but perhaps we should speak English." She then told us that she had learned English when the American Marines were based on Bora Bora during WWII and she had continued to practice speaking English at every opportunity. We then said some reasonable semblance of our thanks and goodbyes.

We resumed our delightful hike to the village with our small crowd of new friends and were escorted to the Gendarmerie, the police station which also served as the customs office. All the boys waited outside and hung through the open windows as we talked with the uniformed French *gendarme,* who looked exactly like Inspector Clouseau. Fortunately, he spoke English and was very friendly, efficient, and helpful.

He initially said that the office was normally closed on Saturday and Sunday, but that he was in the office working on a very complicated reported case of a missing chicken. He said that he had never known of anyone to enter French Polynesia in Bora Bora and he didn't know if that would be allowed, but made a quick short-wave radio call to his superior in Papeete and received approval to clear us, with the understanding that we would routinely check in at the Gendarmerie during our stay in Bora Bora and would eventually clear in with the Customs and Immigration officials in Papeete. Inspector Clouseau then asked to see our shot cards. When we said that the French Consulate in Honolulu had told us that shot cards would not be required, he shrugged and said: "*C'est la vie*, welcome to Polynesie Français. You may strike your quarantine flag. You have *pratique*." He proceeded to make a big show of loudly stamping a small mountain of forms, most of which he threw into the trash can. The boys were impressed with the performance. Inspector Clouseau handed us our *pratique*.

From the Gendarmerie we went to the Banque de Tahiti to exchange some currency. The bank was closed but a friendly gentleman advised us that Magisan Chin Lee, the Chinese store, would accept and exchange American dollars. We managed to purchase a few items and exchange enough money to last the weekend.

Even though it was August 13, the Fête (July 14th Bastille Day celebration) was still going strong. Lots of grass-shack food and beer establishments were set up in a park area near the town wharf, so we found a table at one and consumed a couple of cold Hinano beers. Second only to the sweet taste of rainwater in the ITCZ, that first swallow of cold Hinano was one for the ages.

We could only handle a couple of beers each and had the good sense to pay our bill and bail out of the grass shack, and wander around the village. The combination of the beer, the relief of having *Lille* safely anchored, the friendliness of the Tahitians, the laughter of the children that accompanied us, and the overall great feeling of accomplishment stayed with us all day. We hung out in the village long enough to then attend the nightly dance. The whole town was there to hear the excellent live music and watch the breathtakingly beautiful Tahitian women dance the *tamure*.

We had a couple more Hinanos, but the whole thing was just too much information for me to process. Our world had been 39 feet long for the past month, and every thought and action had been dedicated to *Lille*. John must have felt the same and told me he was headed back to the boat. Marc and I were okay with that, so we got underway, escorted by our convoy of young boys, a group of young women who had just finished basketball practice, and several ugly but happy dogs.

We weaved back and forth down the road to the amusement of our escorts, all laughing, kicking a soccer ball, dribbling a basketball, and laughing some more. We walked past a bungalow where a Tahitian man was preparing his dinner in a coconut husk fire. We tried to say *Ia ora na* to each household, and one lady taught us to properly say *Ia ora oe I teie po,* meaning "Good evening." That helped.

It was apparent that everyone on the island knew each other. We heard lots of stern orders from mothers to young boys, after which everyone, including the mothers, laughed and the boys resumed doing whatever it was that had elicited the mother's stern orders. There was just a tiny sliver of the moon that night, but the stars were incredible and bright enough to reflect off the white coral road.

To our astonishment a young Tahitian woman with a lovely voice started singing a beautiful Beatles song in English, accompanied by her friend singing in French. Others in the crowd and along the route sang and hummed. The boys and dogs stopped messing around, the pace slowed, and everyone eventually went quiet as the young women sang Paul McCartney's line:

The long and winding road
That leads to your door
Will never disappear
I've seen that road before…

We made it back to the dock, fell into *Haze Gray and Underway* and said goodnight to our new friends, paddled out to *Lille,* and collapsed into a dead asleep.

The next morning I woke up with a wonderful hangover. My first thought was: "We did it. We made it to *Somewhere.*" I made a big pot of SNFO (Special Navy Fuel Oil) and sat in the cockpit nursing a cup and reviewing the voyage. While a 37-day passage that should have been completed in 20 days or so was not something to boast about, I felt immense satisfaction in our accomplishment. The longer passage had made for greater adventure and a bunch of life lessons. Yes, that was it! It was an education, one that cannot be attained any other way. A golden opportunity had knocked on our door and we had answered.

The sun rose over Mount Otemanu, and I smelled pancakes cooking in the galley. Marc produced a massive plate of Bisquick pancakes. We had consumed all the maple syrup, but still had the last bit of our Melon Jam. And, we had a can of Anchor tinned butter that we had purchased at Magisan Chin Lee.

After a quick swim to clear our heads and to clean the grass from *Lille's* waterline,

Ah-Ki cooking at his Fête restaurant

we paddled the IBS ashore and spent the entire day walking around the village and try-ing our best to speak our version of Tahitian. It was apparent that Tahitians welcomed and enjoyed our attempts to speak their language, laughing with us as we mangled the words and pronunciation.

We found a grass-shack bar/restaurant for a late-afternoon dinner and formed an immediate and lasting friendship with the proprietor, Monsieur Ah-Ki Mous-inc (renaissance man, philosopher, adroit businessman, conflicted Chinese Tahi-tian, waterman, fisherman, husband, father, chef, opponent of the nuclear testing on Mururoa Atoll, expert on the female form, farmer, dog lover, science fiction aficionado, environmentalist, Vespa owner/driver, coffee connoisseur, and kind and gentle person).

Ah-Ki made a big show of welcoming and seating us and presented each of us with a huge laminated and colorful multi-paged menu, which included Tahitian, Chinese, French, and American dishes with accompanying color photos. He then presented three ice-cold Hinanos, broke out a pad and pencil, and asked in English, "What you like Joe?" John asked about the steak. Ah-Ki replied: "No have steak today." Marc asked about the chicken stir-fry. Ah-Ki replied: "No cook chicken today. Too much work." I asked about the hamburger. Ah-Ki replied: "No have cow today." After several more inquiries to which Ah-Ki responded "*Aita* (No)," we started to get the picture and John asked Ah-Ki to point to something on the menu. Ah-Ki smiled and pointed to the very first item on the menu, which was chow mein, and said, "Ah-Ki chow mein *maitai roa* (very good), you betcha." So, we drank our Hinanos and shared a gigantic platter of very spicy and delicious chow mein. You should consider that we had for the most part been subsisting on the likes of canned Del Monte peas and carrots (no offense toward Del Monte intended), so a platter of spicy chow mein was perfect.

Ah-Ki pulled up a chair and entertained us with fantastic and outrageous stories well into the night, while routinely replenishing our Hinanos and bringing two more overflowing platters of chow mein. We were the only customers the entire evening. A Tahitian band played lovely music in a nearby grass-shack bar.

Like the gracious lady at the roadside fruit stand, Ah-Ki had learned to speak English from the American Marines during World War II and he loved everything about Marite (America). His father was from China and his mother was Tahitian. He struggled mightily with the compelling desire (from his father) to make money and the equally compelling desire (from his mother) to live within the prescriptions of nature. He explained that he wanted to be Tahitian, but due to his Chinese lineage, Tahitian society wanted and expected him to work hard and become a successful businessman. That societal expectation had forced him to open his grass-shack bar/restaurant every year for the Fête, and even though the venture had always been profitable, he realized little joy or satisfaction from the effort. For the remainder of the year he fished, farmed, swam, and enjoyed just living with his family on Bora Bora.

If I understood him correctly, the owner of Magisan Chin Lee was Ah-Ki's cousin and he and Ah-Ki engaged in a constant battle of mores, with the Magisan Chin Lee owner working all day every day and living in the rooms above the store with his family. Ah-Ki worked off and on at Chin Lee but chose to live in a bungalow near the lagoon on the outskirts of the village with his *vahine* (wife) and three children. He had a nice sailing canoe, fished in the morning, and farmed his small *motu* (island on the fringing reef) and his small patch of land on the main island in the afternoon. He said, "My cousin rich man, good for him. I am rich man too, good for me." Somehow, we made it back to the boat that night.

The next day we went to work repairing various components on the boat. A person on another boat told me that Alex, the chief engineer at Hotel Bora Bora, was a top-notch machinist, so I loaded the broken water pump in my backpack and walked the very pleasant 6 kilometers to the hotel and met with Alex. He and his wife Michelle made a tasty lunch, and we talked for a couple of hours. They had sailed from France and planned to make Bora Bora their home and open a yacht club/restaurant. Alex said he could make a partial repair of the water pump but also gave me contact information for a marine supply store in Papeete.

Alex was a ham operator and made a call to Hawaii, and his contact in Hawaii patched me through by phone to a friend with whom I spoke for a few minutes and asked him to call our families to relay our whereabouts.

Back in Vaitape village I went to the Bureau de Poste (*fare rata*) and called the marine supply store. The water pump was not in stock, but I made arrangements for payment and delivery to Bora Bora. The process was surprisingly simple and efficient, and the pump arrived about 10 days later.

One day we rented bicycles and rode around the island. The vista looking out over the lagoon from the southern point of Bora Bora was stunning. We met lots of friendly people as we took our time cruising down the perimeter road, and we made notes of anchorages that we planned to explore in the coming days.

We moved *Lille* to the dock at Faanui Bay and filled our water tanks, and then motored to the Hotel Oa Oa closer to the village and picked up one of the two mooring buoys. We put a couple of coats of spar varnish on the masts, booms, gaffs, rails, hatch covers, and doghouse. We installed the new headstay, removed the broken chainplate, and repaired several other minor problems. *Lille* was looking good. Alex recommended a couple of shops in Papeete where we might be able to get a new chainplate fabricated.

We usually joined the nightly basketball or volleyball game to get some exercise and eyeball a young lady that we reckoned was the World's Most Beautiful Woman. We might have been right. She was also a very good athlete and showed no mercy when spiking a volleyball. I held my own at basketball but was new to volleyball and took some hits. Good fun! Somehow, getting hit square in the face by a spike from the World's Most Beautiful Woman was okay.

For the basketball games, the players took turns being the *arbit* (referee) for the night. When my turn came, I had a hard time conveying in Tahitian the calls for various infractions but managed to get the message across and provided some entertainment, judging by the level of laughter after each call.

We anchored in the lee of Motu Toopua a couple of times. Ah-Ki joined us for the nights at Toopua and kept us laughing. He was a beast in the water, able to hold his breath for minutes and surfacing with a bag full of pahua, a delicious-tasting clam-like mollusk. He taught us which fish were best to spear and which ones might be *aita maitai* (no good), meaning they might have ciguatera poisoning.

Ah-Ki took command of the galley aboard *Lille* and sautéed the pahua in a lime-and-coconut-milk sauce, and we washed it down with Armenian wine that Ah-Ki called *faraqui*. It was hard to understand why the wine in a French country came from Armenia. He also made a big bowl of *ia ota* (*poisson cru*, ceviche) using cubes of parrot fish, *fe'e* (octopus), adding fresh coconut milk, cucumbers, onions, and tomatoes from his garden, and "cooking" the lot in lime juice.

We also made friends with Alain, a Tahitian fellow about our age who was on Bora Bora filling in as manager of Banque de Tahiti, while the regular manager was on vacation. Alain was a good guitar player, and we figured that every woman on Bora Bora was in love with the poor guy. It certainly seemed that way when we saw him at the nightly dances. Alain lived in a bungalow at the Hotel Oa Oa. His Tahitian-English pronunciation sounded like "bangalow," which was appropriate. We met up with him later when we got to Papeete, and it was the same thing at the night clubs, with women hanging all over him. Alain was the grandson of the Chief of Tikehau, one of the atolls in the Tuamotu Archipelago. Alain insisted that we visit Tikehau, and we promised that we would.

Most days, Ah-Ki came to the boat for a breakfast of scrambled eggs, Bisquick pancakes, and various fruits. We still had some eggs that we had brought from Hawaii. Prior to departure, we had boiled each egg for a few seconds to seal the shell and that had really worked. The eggs had never been refrigerated and were still tasty.

Ah-Ki preferred eggs from American chickens. It was a big deal for him. One night when we were at his house for *café* (Ah-Ki referred to dinner as *café*), he said in his wonderful pidgin English dialect: "Whatsa matta Tahitian chicken. Why he eat rocks. I dun know. Marite chicken no eat rocks."

He had observed Tahitian chickens *(Gallus gallus)* picking up pebbles (to aid digestion), but of course had never seen American chickens eat pebbles. He was

Lille anchored in 8 feet of water

bothered by the rock-eating Tahitian chickens but endured them because there was no other option if he wanted to provide chickens and eggs for his family. As I noted earlier, the man was a philosopher, but he was also a realist. I know some will think that I am being unfair to Ah-Ki regarding his dialect, but I assure you that his English was far superior to our Tahitian, which provided him with hours of laughter. Ah-Ki was very patient in his efforts to teach us Tahitian, and in return we taught him some choice American phrases. Unfortunately, we realized too late that we might have gone a bit over the top, when one night after dinner I asked Teraii, Ah-Ki's *vahine*, if there was any more coffee, and she replied: "Fuckin A, Bubba."

We had *café* most nights at Ah-Ki's house. I will always treasure those evenings. We managed to have some very interesting and complicated discussions, while cooking and eating *ma'a Tahiti* (Tahitian food) that he gathered from the waters near his *motu* and from his small plot of land on the slope above his bungalow. We did our best to contribute by bringing sardines, canned Dinty Moore beef stew, and various canned vegetables. *Café* started with a small bowl of *poisson cru*, and then the main course consisting of all kinds of wonderful fruits and vegetables, fish, *maneo po'e* (tapioca pudding), banana *po'e*, *uru* (breadfruit), and sometimes some type of baked seabird. There was always a large pitcher of *pape to'e to'e* (cold water), and then of course after dinner he served very dark and rich coffee with a touch of vanilla bean, both of which were grown at the higher elevations of his property. Alain occasionally joined us for *café*.

One night while finishing the meal with a cup of coffee, Ah-Ki told us about working for the government on the nuclear testing project on Mururoa Atoll in the Tuamotus. He became very emotional and had to stop talking. He said: "No more talk. Bomb *aita maitai*."

We worked with Ah-Ki on his *motu* and on his upslope land, clearing an area and also planting a new crop of *maneo* (*Manihot esculenta*). *Maneo* (tapioca) was a Tahitian dietary staple. Ah-Ki made bread and deep-fried sugary pastries from the *maneo* and *uru* that he harvested.

The new water pump arrived at the Bureau de Poste. We installed it, purchased a few provisions at Magisan Chin Lee, and sailed around to the windward side of the island.

Marc went aloft to direct our navigation around the bommies (random coral patches) on the way to a white-sand-bottom anchorage in about 8 feet of crystal-clear water in the lee of Motu Apomeo. Anchorages just do not get any better! Tidal

Cuttlefish, the world's most weirdly beautiful creature

ranges in the Society Islands are very slight. Therefore, anchoring in that shallow water was not a problem, and *Lille*'s keel brushed the sand at low water.

We dove on the reef outside and speared some good fish. We then spent a few days moving to different anchorages, and managed to run aground on hard sand as we explored the area near Matira Point. The moon was near full. We set a Danforth anchor off the beam in shallow water on the weather side (starboard) and rigged it to the main halyard. We also rigged a Yachtsman anchor straight out from the bow and another Danforth anchor in deeper water to the capstan and through the port bow hawse, and then waited for the next high water. When the boat started feeling lively, we tensioned the halyard and the boat heeled over, just clearing the bottom. We then got up on the Yachtsman and Danforth anchors rigged to the capstan and warped the boat to deeper water as we eased the weather anchor—Bob's your uncle! It was good practice and great fun. A full keel does have a few advantages.

We spent the rest of the night scuba diving and snorkeling the reefs. The lagoon was lit up a dull green and lots of weird animals were out for walkabout. It was like

Halloween night in Lahaina. We caught a few spiny lobsters and saw a school of cuttlefish, colorful and weirdly beautiful.

That night was the first time I witnessed a parrot fish in a cocoon. Parrot fish have glands that secret a mucous biopolymer cocoon that surrounds the fish, protecting it from parasites and allowing the fish to sleep. The cocoon also protects the fish from predators by masking olfactory cues. I found a nice-sized parrot fish in a hole and was about to spear it when I noticed the mysterious cocoon and then made the mistake of poking it. The fish woke up and seemed stunned at first, then exploded out of the cocoon, crashing right into my face plate and coating my mask and head with the gelatinous mess. I don't know which of us was more startled.

We eventually made our way back to the leeward side of Bora Bora. The chart showed a least depth of 1 fathom along our route while still on the windward side. We managed to find that least depth, but by then kedging off was no problem and we were free in a couple of hours.

Ah-Ki drinking from a coconut during Tupai expedition

10

Ah-Ki Adventure

WE GOT BACK to Hotel Oa Oa and found an available mooring buoy. Ah-Ki saw us, waved from the dock, and we took *Haze Gray and Underway* in to retrieve him. He brought along a big bowl of fresh *poisson cru* made with tuna (*bonit*) that his friend Marcel had caught that day. He had a good laugh when we told him about running aground.

John went with Ah-Ki to make bird-catching poles for our planned spearfishing and bird-catching trip to Tupai Atoll the following day.

We got underway at 0700 with Ah-Ki, his *vahine* Teraii, and his friends Marcel and Pua. We had light winds but managed to poop-sail up to the windward side of the atoll.

I stayed aboard *Lille*, slowly sailing around the area, while the others went hunting. Ah-Ki worked out of *Haze Gray and Underway* and caught some birds, while also choreographing the whole show. After a couple of hours John swapped out with me.

Marcel and Pua were amazing divers, able to hang out for two to three minutes at 60 feet and bring up a speared fish on most dives. They were using 6-foot-long, homemade wooden *pupue* (spear guns) that had three arbaletes and stainless-steel spears.

Numerous blacktip and whitetip sharks showed up but were not a problem. The island's fringing reef was etched with sand channels running perpendicular to the reef. The swell surged in and out of the channels. I was in one of the sand channels about 20 feet down, hanging onto a coral ledge during the surge, when a whitetip came blasting out of the channel with the ebb. The shark narrowly missed crashing into me. Scared the hell out of both of us.

All was fine until Ah-Ki got into an argument with the French *patron* (boss) on the island, who yelled from shore that we were not allowed to fish there. At least I think that is what he said. But it was okay because by then we had speared enough fish and Ah-Ki was happy with his bird haul.

We had a pleasant sail back to Bora Bora. Pua mixed up a big bowl of *poisson cru* and we had some iced Hinanos. We were living the good life. Good friends, easy sailing, fresh *poisson cru*, and cold Hinano. When we threw off the docklines back in Hawaii, we imagined that we were in for some good times, but that day surpassed all expectations.

The next day Marcel guided us to the top of Mount Pahia from which the view was magnificent. Marcel pointed out plants along the way and told us how each plant is used for food, medicinal purposes, clothing, building, etc. That afternoon he and Pua gave each of us a *pupue*. We used those spearguns for the rest of the voyage through French Polynesia.

The Fête was done by the end of August, so we helped Ah-Ki tear down his restaurant. As we worked, a gentleman from an English yacht stopped to help and talk for a few minutes. He brought bottles of cold Hinano, and Ah-Ki kept us in rapt attention with his explicit comments about the physical attributes of some of the nearby women yachties. Political correctness was not a strong suit for Ah-Ki. As the Englishman was leaving, he commented about Ah-Ki: "What a delightful chap." Yes indeed! That is how I would always remember Ah-Ki, a delightful chap.

We also helped Alex dismantle and then reassemble one of the grass bungalows on the site of his new yacht club at Faanui. Alex was a very clever builder, and we had the bungalow up in a few hours.

One day after breakfast on the boat, Marcel came alongside in his *pahi iti* (small boat). We loaded aboard and headed out to Motu Tapu, about a half mile south of Passe Teavanui. Marc went with Marcel to gather pahua and John and I helped Ah-Ki lay net. We worked hard until noon when Ah-Ki said, "Okay, we stop, eat, rest, maybe one hour we fish more." He explained that when the sun is high, the fish hide in the coral reef to avoid the heat, so laying net would be a waste of time. We made a fire with coconut husks and cooked some of the catch by laying the whole fish on the coral stones in the fire. The burning coconut husks heated the coral stones and the heat of the stones cooked the fish. Marc and Marcel returned with a mess of pahua, and by beer-thirty we had netted about 50 good fish.

The next day was Tapati (Sunday), and Ah-Ki made a huge *tama'ara'a* (feast) with the food that we had gathered. He cooked the food in the *himaa*, starting the process well before dawn. He had a special collection of *himaa* stones that he had gathered over the years, and *tama'ara'a* was a sacred event for him.

After wrapping all the food in banana leaves and covering the hot stones and wrappings with more banana leaves and a layer of dirt, we had to wait for the food

U.S. Marine Corps WWII *pupue* (cannon), with Toopua in the background

to cook, so Ah-Ki took us up the mountain to see the American *pupue* (cannon), one of the eight artillery guns that the Marines placed on the island during WWII.

The gun pointed out to Passe Teavanui. Ah-Ki was very proud of the *pupue* but was angry with the government for allowing it to rust. He said: "Maybe *pupue* no broke, I shoot crazy French *tane* on Tupai." He was pretending to still be mad at the French *patron* on Tupai Atoll, but he couldn't hold back his wonderful laugh.

We headed down the hill to Ah-Ki's bungalow. All of his smiling-eyed neighbors attended, and everyone brought something to share. His adjacent neighbor cooked a pig in his own *himaa* and made that his contribution. The *tama'ara'a* lasted all night. Several folks showed up with guitars and Tahitian banjos, and there was lots of dancing.

It eventually became time for us to move along on our voyage through French Polynesia. The night before departing for Raiatea, we took Ah-Ki, Teraii, Marcel,

Clay, John, Ah-Ki, and Marc

and Alain to the Oa Oa Restaurant for a very pleasant mahi mahi dinner. Ah-Ki got emotional and said to us, "Maybe you go Hawaii, I no see you." That was hard to hear. The next morning, I checked out with Inspector Clouseau at the Gendarmerie, then walked back to the Hotel Oa Oa dock, where Ah-Ki, Alain, and Marcel met us to say goodbye. Ah-Ki shouted out, "Roll Tide, Ya'll" as we hoisted anchor and departed for Raiatea.

Our time in Bora Bora had been a real learning experience. Some good adventures, new friendships, and a better understanding of human nature.

John, Clay, and Marc anchored in Faaroa Bay, Raiatea

11

Raiatea

WHILE LEAVING OUR Bora Bora friends was difficult, we managed to make a composed departure out of Passe Teavanui and then had very nice sailing conditions for the short trip to Raiatea.

We entered Passe Rautoranui, dropped sails, and motored to the town of Uturoa and anchored in 100 feet. Quite the culture shock. Uturoa was a bustling metropolis compared to Vaitape. We went ashore and checked in with the *gendarme*, who did not look like Inspector Clouseau and said: "Oh, you are the boat that entered French Polynesia in Bora Bora. We were told to expect you, Welcome." I was impressed with the efficiency of the system. It was a comforting to know that someone was actually keeping tabs on our whereabouts.

We strolled around town looking for a hardware store and ran into Frank, a friend from Honolulu, who had just pulled in aboard his nice cold-molded Wylie sloop *Silkie*. He decided to buddy-boat with us the next day down to Faaroa Bay.

We stopped by the Bali Hai Hotel for a lemonade and met Darlene, a lovely young woman also from Honolulu who was on an extended singlehanded back-packing tour of French Polynesia. During our conversation she hinted that she had very recently been through a bad experience of some sort, so we asked her if she wanted to join us on the boat for a few days. She seemed very relieved by the offer, said yes, and proved to be an enthusiastic and worthy shipmate, despite having no prior boating experience. She stayed aboard for the duration of our time in Raiatea and Huahine.

The next day we tried to weigh anchor, but the nylon rode was wrapped around a coral head at 50–60 feet. As luck would have it, our scuba bottles were empty, so we made a few free-dives down to sort out the mess. It could have been a real problem if the rode had been fouled at the bottom.

We got underway for Faaroa Bay, a long and narrow bay on the east side of Raiatea. We anchored in 35 feet with a mud bottom and felt very comfortable after the deep anchorage in Uturoa. Frank anchored nearby, and then we launched the IBS and Frank's dinghy and paddled a couple of kilometers up the river at the head of the bay, through gorgeous scenery. We managed to sail out of the river by rigging our T-shirts to the paddles.

A small group of islanders came out to the boat in an outrigger canoe and stayed until 0300 the next morning playing guitar and singing. Temanu, one of the group, was a wildman and was three sheets to the wind and a bit too rowdy after drinking just a couple of shots of rum. It was obvious that he had a keen interest in the lovely Darlene, so to avoid any trouble, we "escorted" him to the foredeck and laid him down with a pillow and blanket. He went to sleep immediately. The others paddled ashore in their canoe shortly thereafter.

Temanu and *Haze Gray* were gone when we awoke at sunrise. But shortly thereafter we noticed Temanu paddling *Haze Gray* back out to *Lille*. We made a big pot of strong, dark coffee, using roasted beans from Ah-Ki's place, and had a very pleasant and interesting conversation with Temanu. He was a fisherman and surfer and pointed out a few good surf breaks. He stayed aboard until early evening.

That afternoon we climbed the ratlines to the crosstrees and did some fancy diving. John did a cannonball that damn near emptied Faaroa Bay. Temanu did a sort of head-first cannonball that we called a watermelon. I did a back flip. Marc was ready to add a twist to his first front one-and-a-half, and John yelled up, "Hey Marc, do a gainer." Marc responded, "What's a gainer?" John explained that Marc should face outboard and then do a reverse flip. Without hesitation, Marc launched out into space and executed a respectable full gainer. John said, "Marc, I was joking, good grief!" I said to John, "Marc is just like Henry." Henry, our crazy Alabama cousin, had a strange compulsion to do a gainer off of every bridge he met, no matter the height or the season and even if he was fully clothed. And of course I always had to jump in after him to make sure he was okay. Marc's gainer was cool, but he said, "I can do better than that" and started to climb back up to the spreaders. I asked him to wait a minute so that I could go out in *Haze Gray* and get some film of the gainer using Darlene's Super 8 camera.

While Marc waited, Temanu decided that he needed to do a gainer. His effort started out well, but he only completed about 75 percent of the reverse flip and finished with a spectacular belly-buster. He was obviously in pain but managed to laugh it off and went back up for another Olympics-qualifying watermelon. Marc's second gainer was near perfect.

The next day I went ashore and hitched a ride into Uturoa to check out with the *gendarme*. I stopped for lunch at the Meri Meri Restaurant on the waterfront.

Top: Marc is GO for launch
Above: Launch into space

The judges awarded Marc a 9.5 for the dive

An older Tahitian gentleman named Mona joined me and suggested that we share a dish of *inaa*, a fried pancake filled with baby fish. That was interesting, so we then had a plate of chow mein, which also contained baby fish.

Lutz, a German fellow from a nice S&S sloop, and Hinz, a Swiss dude from a weird-looking catamaran, pulled up chairs and shared the chow mein with us. Hinz provided a very colorful story of the two of them singlehanding their boats in tandem from Panama. The leg from Panama to the Marquesas lasted 88 days, 33 of which were spent becalmed within the same 5-square-mile area. Some guys have all the luck!

I walked back to Faaroa Bay, and John paddled *Haze Gray* ashore to retrieve me. We weighed anchor and moved *Lille* to the lee of Motu Taoru in Passe Teavapiti, a surf break recommended by Temanu. We enjoyed some real nice 2–3-foot waves on the outside reef, our first surfing in several months. It was an outstandingly scenic surf spot. We could see Bora Bora, Tahaa, Raiatea, and Huahine.

Marc did some free-diving among the sharks in the pass, and Darlene collected shells on the beach. We remained there for the night and then departed for Huahine at 0600. I think that *Lille* was enjoying having another female aboard. Marc, John, and I had to clean up our acts a bit, and the whole show was better for it.

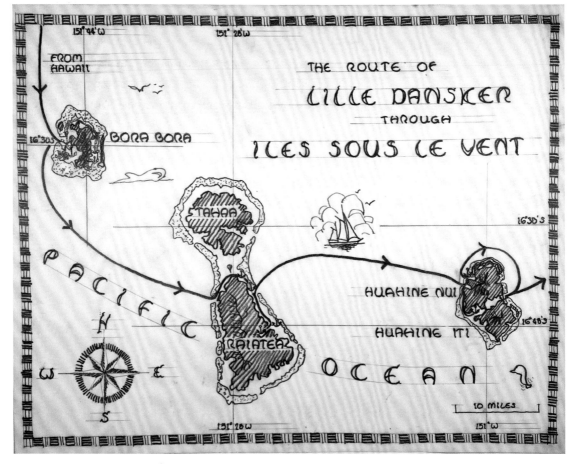

Our route through Îles Sous Le Vente

12

Huahine

W<small>E HAD GOOD WIND</small> out of the south for most of the 22-nautical-mile sail to Huahine, but we ran into a heavy squall as we approached the entrance to Passe Avapehi. We managed to carry full sail as we blasted through the channel, and the squall passed shortly after we entered the lagoon. We motored up to Fare Village, where we had to anchor in the main channel because the preferred anchorage near the Bali Hai Hotel was crowded. The wind got up again and it was a rolly anchorage.

We paddled ashore and checked in with the Huahine *gendarme*, who did not look like Inspector Clouseau either. We all paddled *Haze Gray* out to Passe Avamoa, where John and I surfed some small waves on the famous Huahine left on the south side of the pass. Marc speared some fish and Darlene swam. After a few real sweet rides, I hit my head on the reef, and we all decided that the blood-filled water was probably not a good place to be. The air was cold with the strong south wind anyway, so we headed back to the boat where Darlene announced that it was her turn in the galley. She prepared a fabulous dinner using the fish that Marc had speared.

The next morning, we went ashore to mail some letters at the *fare rata* (Bureau de Poste) and caught a ride in a sort of troop-carrier jeep with five French Army soldiers. We ended up spending the whole day with them and drove all the way around Huahine Nui and Huahine Iti, where we found a quiet restaurant for lunch.

The soldiers were taking some vacation time from duties on Mururoa Atoll, where they were part of the nuclear testing program. They came for dinner on the boat that night and we had a good long talk about their work on Mururoa, the military in general, and life in France. One of the guys was a real comedian but spoke no English. Darlene spoke a bit of French and a couple of the other French guys spoke English, but politely deferred to Darlene as she translated. Everyone had fun trying to interpret some of the semi-translated wild stuff the French comedian said. The evening was a pleasant reminder that people are the same everywhere and just want to get along and have pleasant conversation.

Incognito, one of the boats in the anchorage, had a compressor aboard and the owner Steve offered to fill our scuba bottles. It was a big relief to have the scuba option again after that minor anchor-recovery fiasco in Uturoa.

We motored down the inside passage to Haapu Bay, a very secure anchorage on the west side of Huahine Iti. We were the only boat and dropped anchor in 40 feet.

We hiked to the peak overlooking the bay. On the way down we stopped at Haapu village, a pristine little place with well-maintained homes, manicured yards, and smiling friendly people. We were able to trade canned sardines for a variety of fruits and vegetables, including some papayas that were the size of footballs. The folks were happy to give us as much fruit as we could carry in our backpacks. Marc made a yoke with a piece of hibiscus branch (*Hibiscus rosa-sinensis*) and lugged two stalks of bananas back to the boat.

We found Huahine a very lush and vibrant island, more so than Bora Bora and Raiatea, and the walk along the coral road was very pleasant.

We remained in the anchorage for a couple of days, getting boat maintenance chores done, then caught a light southerly for the sail back up the inside passage to Fare. We pulled alongside the dock and took on water and 15 gallons of diesel, then moved to the anchorage and dropped in 20 feet.

A runabout full of American tourists pulled alongside and we invited everyone aboard. They stayed for a few hours discussing the places they had visited in Tahiti and asking about our voyage. They told us to be sure to go to Tautira village on Tahiti Iti.

Darlene treated us to Sunday brunch at Hotel Bali Hai. The group of Americans from the previous night was sitting at an adjacent table. John is a keen observer of details, and while studying the menu he conferred with Darlene who agreed that it read something like "Choose whatever you want from each course." He then asked the waitress if that meant that he could order everything on the menu for the price of a single brunch. The waitress started laughing like it was the funniest thing she had ever heard and then said, "But of course" and scurried away to gather the other waitresses to see the crazy American sailor who had ordered everything on the menu. They and the crowd of American tourists gathered around and watched John work. It was like Cool Hand Luke eating the 50 hardboiled eggs. To John's credit, he damn near cleaned his plate(s), but later suffered mightily for the effort.

The following day we weighed anchor, exited Passe Avamoa, and sailed over the top of Huahine to the east side, entering Maroe Bay via Passe Farerea.

As luck would have it, the waitresses from Hotel Bali Hai were on the small *motu* just inside Maroe Bay and they were putting on a luau for the group of American tourists. The waitresses flagged us down, so we dropped sails and motored in as close as the reef would allow. Don, one of the American tourists, paddled a canoe out and handed us a thatched basket full of cold Hinanos and fried chicken. That was unexpected, but what really nailed us was when all the waitresses dropped their *pareus* and started dancing on the beach and waving for us to come get them. Darlene pretended to be shocked by the brazenness. Frankly, it was a bit unnerving to see half a dozen beautiful naked women dancing on the beach, and I almost ran the boat aground. Tahitian women can be a caution. But they got a big kick out of teasing us, got dressed, and went back to their luau duties. Don, the only bachelor in the tourist group, for some reason appeared to be extremely anxious to get back to the party and he shoved off.

We continued down to the lee of a large *motu* and anchored in 9 feet of crystal-clear water and hard white sand bottom. That night the moon was a waxing crescent and the stars were as bright as I had ever seen. The sky was reflected on the lagoon and the scene was very confusing, making it difficult to distinguish up from down. Now and then the stars would reflect off the white sand bottom. I had to sit down and close my eyes.

We remained there for a few days diving on the reefs, swimming, hiking the trails onshore, and reading. We walked 7 kilometers for dinner at the restaurant that we had visited with the French Army guys. We didn't see any cars the entire 14-kilometer round trip. And we filled our backpacks with bananas and various fruit from the offerings of folks along the route. We had learned that bananas onboard a boat are okay in Tahiti. (In Hawaii, bananas onboard are bad luck for fishing.)

Darlene had to fly to Papeete to update her travel visa, so we took her ashore and she caught a ride to the Huahine airport. She planned to rejoin us later in Moorea.

We got underway for the 80-nautical-mile overnight trip to Moorea, and as we were abeam the small *motu* in the pass, three of the Hotel Bali Hai waitresses were there preparing for another luau and proceeded to torture us again. We turned the boat in towards them and they screamed, gathered their *pareus*, and ran into the cover of the coconut trees. Naked women—you can't live with 'em; you can live without 'em.

John with fe'e

13

Moorea

W E HAD NEAR-PERFECT close-reaching conditions with almost flat seas and 12–15-knot southerly wind. We had a big dinner of beans and rice and then set the night watch. It felt good to be back out on the ocean at night. *Lille* rejoiced in the conditions as well and kicked up her heels.

I thoroughly enjoyed my 0200–0600 watch with the stars guiding us towards Opunohu Bay, a very deep cut into the north side of Moorea.

We sailed into the bay and dropped in a small embayment on the western shore, next to an old gaff-rigged schooner and near *Hathor*, a nice little but partially dismasted double-ender. We paddled over and visited with Woody, the owner, and learned that he had been dismasted in early January when he was about 2,000 miles east of the Marquesas and then sailed jury-rigged to Tahiti. He was waiting for a new mast.

The valley at the head of Opunohu Bay is a Garden of Eden bordered on three sides by steep cliffs. We hiked into the valley to tour the farms. The lushness was incredible, and we saw dozens of species of fruits, vegetables, and trees. My favorite was the *pamplemousse* (grapefruit, *Citrus maximus*). It seemed like the valley was the perfect growing environment.

Darlene arrived the next morning. She had taken the ferry over from Papeete, hitched a ride along the shore until she found *Lille* anchored in Opunohu Bay, and then whistled from shore for us to come get her. We were happy to see her smiling face.

We all walked up the road to a small roadside grocery/bar and had a cold Coke while sitting under a kamani tree and talking Tahitian with the old couple that owned the place. They invited us into the house, and we sat down and had fun watching a French-dubbed version of *Our Man Flint*.

When we got back to the boat, a Tahitian girl swam out and climbed aboard. Turned out she was from Bora Bora and recognized *Lille* and wanted to say hello. Of course, she knew Ah-Ki and said that she would give him our regards when she returned to Bora Bora.

Opunohu Bay, Moorea

her bow dead into the wind. What a good girl. That reef was just too damn close. Murphy showed up right then when I pushed the engine starter button—no go. John was on it and got the jib up and backed it while I trimmed the main and mizzen. John also made the anchor ready to run. We slowly bore off enough to gather way and claw our way back to weather, short-tacking to open water with Marc's guidance. I tried the engine again and it started. It was just another of those frequent trials that are part of sailing.

To regain *Lille*'s confidence and to show our contempt for Murphy, we did not engage the engine and sailed back up the lagoon and into our anchorage, luffed into the wind, came to a stop, and dropped spot-on. We launched *Haze Gray* and ran a stern line ashore and secured it to a coconut tree, then pulled the stern close to the shore.

Later, as we were sitting in the cockpit discussing how close we had come to losing *Lille* and trying to regain our composure, Darlene said, "You guys really work well together." That was a huge compliment, and we were then able to relax.

We decided to visit Club Med by walking down the road. While we were walking, a Tahitian girl named Tina riding a Vespa stopped to say hello. We took turns pushing Tina's Vespa as she walked along with us. She lived next door to Club Med, knew all the Club Med employees, and escorted us into the place, where we were served champagne and caviar, followed by a fine meal.

It seemed like Club Med welcomed sailors for the purpose of adding a little flavor to the atmosphere. I'm not sure we added much flavor, but we certainly appreciated the hospitality. Tina told us that she worked in Papeete and would like to take us dancing and surfing once we got there. Of course, she knew Alain and said "*OOOh-La-La*" and rolled her eyes.

Darlene's visit to French Polynesia came to an end, so we all hitched a ride to the ferry terminal in the main village and saw her off. Darlene was an intelligent, interesting, and valued shipmate, and I think she enjoyed her time aboard.

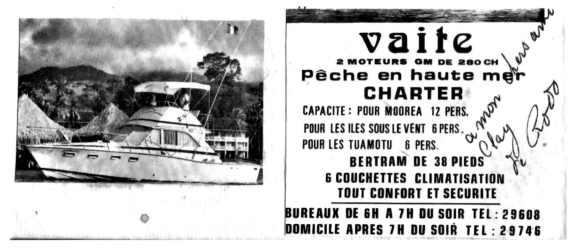

Rodo's charter boat *Vaite*

14

Papeete

W E STAYED AT THE ANCHORAGE in Opunohu Bay until October 4 and then sailed across the channel between Moorea and Tahiti to Papeete, where we "Tahiti-moored" right in the middle of town with a bow anchor in the fairway and a stern line to a bollard onshore. Les and Caroline, friends aboard *Sea Rover* from the Ala Wai Harbor in Honolulu, handled our stern line.

We cleared Customs and Immigration, where the *gendarme* was Inspector Clouseau. He had been promoted to Chief Inspector and reassigned to Papeete. It was great fun to talk with him again, and we congratulated him on his promotion. Chief Inspector Clouseau was genuinely interested to know if we were enjoying our time in French Polynesia. He then handed me a huge package of mail. For some reason, the Bureau de Poste had delivered our mail to the customs office.

I made mooring arrangements with the port captain and headed back to the boat where we dove into the package of mail, finding lots of dated letters from our families wondering where the hell we were. Turned out that not hearing from us for over 40 days had been disturbing for them. Go figure. We had told them to send letters to us at Yacht *Lille Dansker*, General Delivery Papeete, Tahiti, French Polynesia.

The next morning, we walked to Banque de Tahiti and shanghaied Alain, who had returned from his temporary responsibilities at the Bora Bora branch. We walked to a restaurant that served "American Style Hamburgers." The burgers were excellent—I think. They were the only hamburgers we had eaten in a couple of months, so that made them excellent.

Alain decided to take the rest of the day off and escorted us on a walking tour of downtown Papeete. During the tour, John asked Alain if he knew of a man named Rodo Williams and Alain responded, "But of course, everyone knows Rodo, I will take you to his boat." We found Rodo aboard his 38-foot sportfishing charter boat *Vaite*, which was moored next to *Varua*, William Albert *Robinson*'s beautiful Starling Burgess–designed brigantine.

We had been advised by a friend in Hawaii to seek out Mr. Williams if we needed any help while in Tahiti. Our friend told us that Rodo had been a crew member aboard the double-hulled canoe *Hokule'a* on the 1976 voyage between Hawaii and Tahiti.

We talked for a couple of hours with Rodo and then he asked to visit *Lille Dansker*, which was just a short walk down the waterfront. After a tour of the boat, we piled into Rodo's 1956 Deux Cheveaux and drove to a metal fabrication shop to get a new chainplate made for *Lille*'s mizzen shroud. The shop was very organized and well stocked with stainless-steel flatbar. The machinist asked a few questions in French; Rodo translated and negotiated a reasonable price. The fabrication was well made and completed within a few days.

We treated Alain and Rodo to dinner at a quiet side-street bistro, downed a few Hinanos, and continued our interesting conversation, speaking mostly Tahitian. Both Rodo and Alain spoke flawless English and corrected our Tahitian as needed. Rodo talked about the *Hokule'a* voyage and explained that his position aboard *Hokule'a* was to assist the "wayfinder" (navigator) during the long voyage and to serve as pilot once the canoe approached the Tuamotus. Pius "Mau" Piailug, from the island of Satawal in Micronesia, was the wayfinder and he was also assisted by Dr. David Lewis. Each of these three gentlemen had acquired unique abilities in guiding sailing vessels across oceans using natural methods handed down through countless generations and without the use of modern navigation instruments.

Rodo explained to us that in 1976, as the voyaging canoe approached the islands of Polynesia, the southeasterly swell diminished abruptly and then two *itata'e* (white terns) were sighted. Just before sunset the birds stopped fishing and flew southeast. Rodo notified Mau that *Hokule'a* would soon make landfall at Mataiva, Tuamotus. Sure enough, at 0300 the next morning they ghosted into the lee of Mataiva Atoll, the northwestern-most atoll in the Tuamotu Archipelago, located about 170 nautical miles northeast by north of Papeete.

Rodo knew that the southeasterly swell would diminish as they sailed in the huge lee of the archipelago, and he also knew that *itata'e* typically did not venture more than 30 miles from the nest. Rodo explained that distances were discussed and gauged by wayfinders as sailing time. (I reference miles to simplify the picture for those readers with a Western thinking bent, myself included.) *Hokule'a*, her name the Hawaiian name for the star Arcturus, was conceived and constructed in hopes of reviving the ancient Polynesian art and science of voyaging and wayfinding.

The initial round-trip voyage from Hawaii to Tahiti started a renaissance of the almost-lost art. The voyage was somewhat of a miracle in that it revived the pride and the voyaging-related cultural practices of the Polynesian people throughout the Pacific. It created a rebirth of navigating without the use of instruments by using only the wayfinding clues provided by nature. In 1976 there were only a few way-finders still alive in the Pacific, and the Polynesian Voyaging Society located and convinced Mau Piaulug, Dr. David Lewis, and Rodo to join *Hokule'a* and mentor young Hawaiian sailors to learn the incredibly complicated details of wayfinding. While there were numerous challenges, the voyage was a huge success and *Hokule'a* was welcomed by thousands of joyous and cheering Tahitians when she arrived in Papeete on June 4, 1976. (An excellent source for information about the Polynesian voyaging rebirth is *Hawaiki Rising: Hokule'a, Nainoa Thompson, and the Hawaiian Renaissance*, by Dr. Sam Low.)

Alain prompted Rodo to give us some personal background, and we learned that Rodo was descended from an English whaling ship captain, who was ship-wrecked on a Tahiti reef. Rodo had been the skipper of a copra schooner for many years sailing throughout the Tuamotus without the use of instruments. He spoke six languages, was educated as a botanist, specializing in hybrid breadfruit, and fought with the French Army in Vietnam. I felt privileged to speak with Mr. Williams, and cherished the opportunity.

Rodo told us a story about how as a young man he paddled his canoe outside the reef one night to fish. The moon was full and suddenly a tiger shark, longer than the canoe, surfaced next to the canoe, rolled onto her side, and stared at Rodo. The shark stayed alongside all the way back into the lagoon, continuing to stare. Rodo said that when he arose the next morning and looked at himself in the mirror, his hair had turned white.

Rodo graciously offered us the use of his Deux Cheveaux anytime on the condition that we not drive it into the ocean. That was a bit confusing, but we agreed to do our best. He said that he always left the key in the ignition, and we figured the car was community property. Perhaps one of the community drivers had tried to use the Deux Cheveaux as a bateau.

Le Truck

15

Le Truck Voyage

TINA RETURNED from Moorea, found us aboard *Lille* on a Saturday afternoon, and asked us to meet her at Pitate Bar that night, where Jean Gabilou and his band would be performing.

Folks from all over the island arrived in Papeete on Saturdays to go to bars and dance and then go to the open market on Sunday morning. The notorious Quinn's Bar had recently burned down, but most locals reckoned Pitate Bar to be a worthy match.

Shortly after we arrived, we ran into Mahana and Tiarehere, two young women from Bora Bora with whom we had played basketball and volleyball. The music was excellent, but I am not much of a dancer and never was able to get the hang of that quick-step waltz kind of dance, similar to the Texas two-step.

We stayed at Pitate Bar until 0400, when the place was still going strong, and then walked to the open market. Just being in the market was excellent entertainment. Many Tahiti and Moorea residents would go to the Sunday-morning market for fresh produce and every sort of household necessity. The market was huge and had two floors. We stocked up on fresh produce and some locally made gifts to take home.

We noticed a long line of buses on the street, and Tina insisted that a voyage on *Le Truck* was an absolute must. We ran back to the boat, off-loaded our market goods, got our surfboards, ran back to the bus loading area, signed the ship's articles, and joined Tina, Mahana, and Tiarehere in a long line of passengers waiting to board one of the *Le Trucks* in the circle island fleet.

When we made it to the front of the line, we loaded our surfboards on the roof with plans to disembark at Papara. We had been told that there was a good break in the pass leading into Papara.

Our *Le Truck* was a teal and yellow beauty with lots of bangles and such. Her Plimsoll mark was submerged with people, produce, and dozens of woven baskets filled with baguettes wrapped in the sports section of old issues of *The Paris Gazette*. The passenger manifest included several awful-looking but polite Tahitian-speaking dogs (*Canis familiaris*) tethered on the roof, a few smallish French-speaking pigs (*Sus domesticus*) occupying seats, lots of rock-eating chickens lashed to and hanging out of the windows, flapping in the breeze, and stringers of fish hanging from the boarding ladders. Several people had guitars and Tahitian ukuleles, one gentleman had a washboard, and another fellow had a washtub bass that he set up in the bow next to the skipper. Everyone, including the skipper and the pigs, had been up all night dancing at one of the clubs. We were still slightly drunk and maybe a bit hungover, and it felt good to take a seat, relax, and witness the proceedings.

The music and singing had started while we were in line and continued nonstop. Some of the women managed to find room in the aisle to dance *tamure*. A lady put a *pareu* and a *lauhala* hat on the pig occupying the seat next to me on my starboard side, and when the pig saw the women dancing, she jumped down and joined in.

Our leg of the voyage was only about 25 miles, but we routinely stopped to off-load and board passengers and made a few side trips to stores for items that some of the passengers had forgotten to buy at the market. The side trips were just an excuse to say hello to friends. The skipper seemed to know each passenger by name and soon learned our names. He and the pigs disembarked at each stop to stretch legs and commune with neighbors. The skipper must have gotten confused after the second stop and when we had weighed anchor, he put the helm hard to port and headed nor'west by west along the road back towards Papeete. Fortunately, the skipper of the Tail-End Charlie *Le Truck* in the convoy was headed sou'east by east and signaled for us to turn around. Skipper got us squared away and headed back in the right direction. There was very little traffic along the route.

An older gentleman sitting next to me on my port side continuously bellowed some nonsense that approximated a song until he finally passed out face-down in the lap of a *pareu*-clad woman sitting on the opposing row of wooden bench seats. Somehow, at the last stop, he came to with a smile on his face, stood up, let out a stupendous belch, staggered off *Le Truck*, and went into the store to purchase another 650-ml Hinano. Unfortunately, he got back on the wrong *Le Truck*, one that was headed nor'west by west, back to Papeete.

When we arrived at Papara village, the skipper agreed to take us down to the beachfront where everyone, including the skipper and the pigs, bailed out, where-upon the skipper announced that he needed to take a nap. There was no objection, so everyone laid down in the shade of a big *kamani* tree (*Calophyllum inophyllum*) while we headed out into the surf.

We had a good session in head-high waves. Nothing like a decent surf session complete with a few wipeouts to clear the cobwebs. After paddling back to shore we found everyone, including the skipper and the pigs, under the *kamani* tree, singing, accompanied by the guitar, ukulele, washboard, and washtub bass musicians.

Eventually everyone loaded up and the skipper drove up to the main intersection in the village, where we disembarked, grabbed our boards, said goodbye to our shipmates, and were able to flag down a Papeete-bound *Le Truck*. Tina, Mahana, and Tiarehere went with us, and at the last moment the pig in the *pareu* and *lauhala* hat climbed aboard our Papeete-bound vessel and sat down next to me. I think she had taken a shine to me.

We finished our boat projects thanks in great part to Rodo's assistance. He seemed to enjoy being able to help. That was typical of the Tahitian people in general. We certainly appreciated the help and enjoyed his company. Very interesting fellow—another delightful chap.

Tina offered to take us for a ride around Tahiti Nui and Tahiti Iti and suggested that we bring our boards. She drove an ancient VW Beetle, and we lashed the boards to the roof. The car was a marvel. The clutch was not functioning, so shifting required finding the optimum upshift or downshift sweet spot, letting off the throttle, and then easing the stick until the gears meshed.

Despite the questionable mechanical condition of the car, Tina had splurged and installed a good cassette sound system. Cranking the volume up to ear-bleed level negated the gear grinding sounds. She had a random mix of cassettes, mostly in French, but she had recently purchased the Eagles' new album, *Hotel California*. We were doing just fine enjoying the music and grinding our way down the road towards Tahiti Iti when the title song came on. During the extended electric guitar ending of the song, Tina pulled to the side of the road, turned off the cassette player, and asked, "How does he do that?"

At first, I didn't know what she was asking but then realized that she was asking how one guitar player could play that incredible solo. Having only recently heard the song for the first time, I hadn't considered that but then wondered, "How the heck does he do that?" It wasn't until months later in Hawaii that I learned that Don Felder and Joe Walsh were working together to produce that wondrous sound. Tina might still be thinking that American guitar players are superhuman.

We stopped briefly at the Paul Gauguin museum and after just a few minutes decided that we needed to come back when we had more time to really appreciate

Le Truck, 1952

the place. Tina told us that the museum contained several of Gauguin's originals that he had painted while living in Tahiti. From there we headed down to Teahupo'o village to check out the surf out on the reef.

Even though the Teahupo'o waves were very small that day, we only watched and then confessed to Tina that there was no way we were going out in that surf. That break was way too fast and well beyond our abilities, and anyway it would have been a very long paddle out to the break. Quoting Clint Eastwood, "A man has got to know his limitations."

We climbed back aboard the VW bug, backtracked to Taravao, and carried on to the village of Tautira on Tahiti Iti, where we found a nice little bungalow restaurant and had lunch, followed by a walking tour of the village. Of all the villages that we visited in the Society Islands, Tautira was my favorite. We got a good look at Tautira Bay (Cook's Anchorage) and resolved to eventually anchor there.

We headed back to Tahiti Nui and continued along the north coast back to Papeete, stopping at Point Venus, where James Cook established a fort and set up his instruments to observe the transit of Venus in 1769.

Point Venus Lighthouse

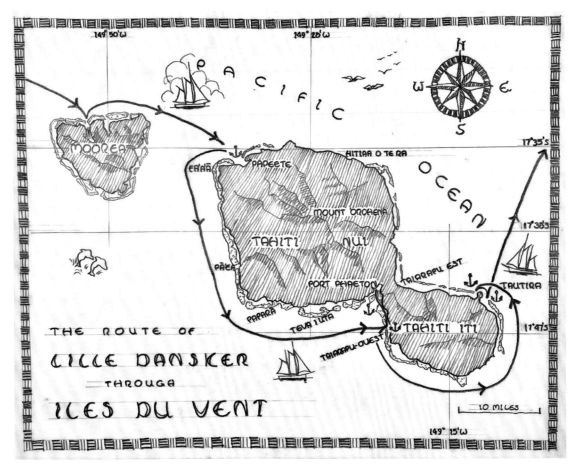

Our anchorages in Îles Du Vent

16

Tautira Village

W E REALIZED that we were spending far too much time sequestered in the comforts of Papeete and needed to cast off the lines and get back to the real world of voyaging. We stocked up on provisions at the Chinese store, shifted to the fuel pier to top-off, and said goodbyes to Rodo, Alain, Tina, and others. Alain handed me an envelope that contained a letter introducing us to his grandfather, the Chief of Tikehau. We departed Papeete Harbor and headed for Tahiti Iti.

Initially we sailed in strong trades with a reef in the main and mizzen, but the wind gradually eased as we worked our way to Tapuaeraha Pass on the northwest coast of Tahiti Iti and eventually found a less-than-perfect anchorage in 8 fathoms near the Oceanographic Research Office.

We were surprised at how tired we were after a day of sailing. It hadn't taken long to get out of shape. Marc made a delicious meal of fresh eggplant, potatoes, and other vegetables. A squall moved through during the night, and I awoke to find myself totally drenched after sleepwalking on the foredeck trying to drop the furled jib. John met me at the base of the companionway ladder and asked what I was doing. I told him that I was just checking things. That was odd, but even though we were anchored, it felt good to be back in the game. It was literally and figuratively a wake-up call. Put me in, Coach!

I stayed up for the remainder of the night studying the upcoming leg between Tahiti and the Tuamotus. There were countless stories of boats being lost on the reefs of the atolls. I wanted to start the leg in favorable conditions that could provide reasonable assurance of a high-sun landfall. And, we had become more cautious following our close encounter with the reef at Moorea.

I assembled a plan for a route from Tautira to Tikehau and would later brief John and Marc on the details. They were good about wanting to know the big picture and the details. During the sail down from Hawaii we had made an all-hands practice of reviewing the daily progress and upcoming conditions, and it was more important than ever to continue that practice.

We motored up the inside passage to Port Phaeton in the isthmus between Tahiti

Marc on lookout as we sailed into Port Phaeton

Nui and Tahiti Iti, known as one of the most secure anchorages in French Polynesia.

Somehow Tina knew that we were there and showed up on shore. Perhaps she had heard it through the Coconut Wireless. She took us back to the Gauguin museum for a real visit. Tina always kept us laughing. She was a splendid person.

After a couple of days at anchor, allowing a frontal system to clear, we motored back down to Taupuaeraha Pass and headed out for Tautira on the north shore of Tahiti Iti.

We experienced a magnificent green flash as we sailed out of the pass. For doubters, a green flash is a real thing with logical science to back it up. I have only seen the green flash a few times, but each time is a wonder. I always interpret things like a green flash or rainbows or dolphins on the bow as good karma, so we were in for a good sail to Tautira. I was on watch at about 2300 when a meteor with an incredibly long tail crossed our bow. More good karma.

We arrived outside Tautira Bay well before dawn, so we hove-to and waited for sunrise. It had been a very pleasant and leisurely sail. The view of Tahiti Iti from offshore was spectacular. Once we had adequate light, we motored into Tautira Bay and anchored in 20 feet of water with a black sand bottom.

We had intended to leave for Tikehau as soon as the weather was favorable. So, on the morning we arrived we went ashore to call Chief Inspector Clouseau to give him an update.

While wandering through the village we met some villagers (Victor, Henri, Tabu, and Vivi) at a roadside thatched bamboo restaurant. Okay, those guys were hilarious. Victor Clark, also known as Vito or Pirae, was the chief spokesman and official comic/troublemaker. He was Tahiti's Rodney Dangerfield. When he learned that we were from Hawaii, he said that "Maire Nui," the outrigger canoe team from Tautira, was returning soon from the annual Molokai Channel Race in Hawaii. Victor had paddled in that race several years before. He also told us that *Hokule'a* had anchored in Tautira Bay the year before. Vivi was the champion *bonit* fisherman and could land two big tuna at the same time with a pole in each hand. Henri was the *mutoi* (sheriff) of Tautira, and his friends called him Mutoi.

To avoid confusion, we settled on Pirae for Victor's name. He asked where we were headed from Tautira. When we told him that we planned to leave soon for Tikehau, he went quiet for a minute and then said: "*Aita maitai*, moon full *ananahi* (tomorrow), wait ten days." We had been in the islands long enough by then to listen to and consider any local advice related to the ocean. I usually like having a full moon during a passage; that makes the night watches easier and provides some light to see islands and other obstructions. But Pirae's insistence was notable. He explained that in ten days the wind would clock from northeast to southeast and would be moderate, and we would have a good sail to Tikehau. He said that he had made the voyage a few times. Tikehau is 175 nautical miles from Tautira on a true course of 016, so a moderate southeast wind would be perfect.

Pirae then told us that anchoring in Tautira Bay was not good in the current weather conditions and that we should move around to the east side of the peninsula. I can't say that we were totally convinced with Pirae's advice about that, because the bay seemed to be an excellent anchorage. We decided to stay anchored where we were. But that night did the job and convinced us that Pirae knew his stuff, when at about 0200 the wind got up to "Hugest" (that category should be an addition to the Beaufort Scale), and the rain came down like we were standing under Niagara Falls.

Lille anchored in Tautira Bay

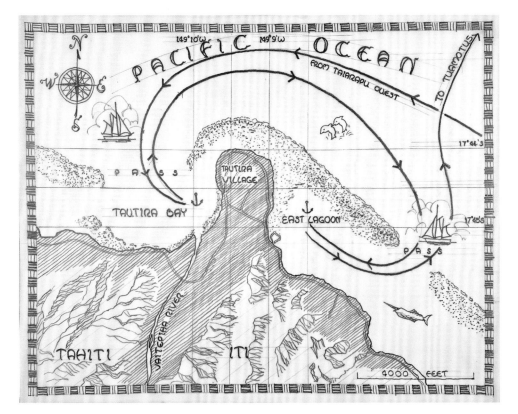

Tautira village and anchorages

We were anchored near the mouth of the Vaitepiha River, and with all the rain, the river that extends far up into the valley had swelled and was raging out into the bay opposing the north-northeast wind. We started dragging. Yes, of course Murphy made an unwelcome appearance—the compass light didn't work and the flashlight batteries were dead. Marc jumped below to refresh the batteries. Just before he returned, our good karma trumped Murphy when lightning struck a tree nearby onshore and set the tree ablaze, briefly lighting up the bay enough for us to determine where we were and how to get the hell out of there. But we came dangerously close to a reef and realized that we could not get out of the bay safely. We decided to re-anchor further out in the bay. It took three attempts before the anchor grabbed.

We stayed in the cockpit with the engine slow ahead into the river current and stern to the wind. It was a very strange and confusing orientation. I had to close my eyes now and then to mentally visualize what nature was doing. That was a good lesson about the power of water current. Once we had enough light to see, we

Breadfruit

noticed that our anchor rode was snubbed on a coral head. Marc dove right in and unfouled it.

Pirae flagged us down from the beach shortly after dawn, and we paddled *Haze Gray* in to get him. He laughed and said that he thought we must have had an interesting night. His laughter soothed the tension that we were feeling. Tahitians have a wonderful outlook on life and manage to laugh at almost everything.

Pirae stayed aboard while we sailed out of the bay. The wind had backed a bit to north and had dropped to about 20–25 knots. The wind direction was favorable for a beam reach out and back, so we decided to go for a sail and held port tack for an hour or so, jibed around, and reached back to the anchorage that Pirae had recommended on the east side of the village. When we arrived at the pass, Pirae climbed

Standing: Clay, Pirae, Mutoi, Vivi. Seated: Tina and Pam

partway up the starboard ratlines and piloted us through and into the anchorage tucked in behind the reef. It was obvious that Pirae was a sailor and was comfortable on boats. He was a competent and pleasant crewman, and it appeared that he thoroughly enjoyed the sail.

There were dozens of waterfalls cascading into the valley off the cliffs behind the village. Some of the higher waterfalls were being blown into clouds by the updraft of the strong wind and never reached the floor of the valley. We had seen that same phenomenon on the north shore of Molokai.

Even though the new anchorage was deep and on the windward side during northeast–southeast trade winds, the reef afforded good protection and the holding was good. Pirae said we should stay there until departing for Tikehau. We took his advice, and it worked out well. Local knowledge almost always helps.

We went to Pirae's house that afternoon. On the way we stopped at the

Chinese store and called Chief Inspector Clouseau, Rodo, Tina, and Alain to let them know that we would be staying in Tautira for a while.

Pirae had a lush garden that included many of the common Tahitian fruits and vegetables. He also had chickens and a couple of pigs. His dietary staple was breadfruit (*Artocarpus altilis*), and he had planted several of those beautiful trees around the property, creating a park-like setting.

After touring Pirae's garden, we stayed for dinner, served on a table set up beneath the largest breadfruit tree. Pirae and his *vahine*, Tiria, were gracious hosts and, typical of Tahitians, waited to eat until we had finished.

After the meal, Pirae took us inside the house and proudly demonstrated his *automatique* door. He had recently installed a swinging door between the kitchen and the main room and realized after the fact that when the door was swung fully open, it closed the open doorway between the main room and the bedroom. *Automatique!!!* Each of us had to open and close the door several times while announcing *"Automatique."* Pirae laughed until he cried. It was Ah-Ki all over again.

Later that evening Pirae told us that Captain Cook's anchor was somewhere in Tautira Bay. The next day Rodo showed up in the Deux Cheveaux. He had stopped by Tina's workplace, and she arranged to take a couple of days off and came with him. Rodo knew a lot of folks in Tautira. They all knew of him.

Pirae and Rodo talked about Cook's anchor, launched two canoes, and we all went out into Cooks Bay and dove on the spot where they reckoned we would find the anchor. We had great fun not finding the anchor. Tina brought her Polaroid camera and took group photos that Pirae put on a window ledge in his house.

Rodo and Tina stayed aboard *Lille Dansker* for a couple of days. We all hiked up into the valley alongside the Vaitepiha River to gather fruit, and we bathed in the river.

Pirae, Tiria, and Mutoi came to the boat for dinner, and I think that with the help of Tina and Rodo, we did a commendable job of producing a tasty Tahitian meal of fruits, vegetables, and seafood that we had gathered.

Two of Pirae's sons brought guitars to the boat later, and the music lasted well into the early morning. Singing is a big part of life in Tautira. We spoke only Tahitian that night and somehow managed to understand each other, provided the conversation was limited to the ocean, women, boats, beer, women, fishing, women, and food. Isn't that all there is to life anyway?

Mutoi really got into the music (and beer) and jumped up and started dancing a sort of Charleston *tamure*. He would get a bit crazy, and Pirae would put his hand

John at the Vaitepiha River, Tautira

on Mutoi's shoulder and say, "*Haere maru*, Mutoi, *haere maru*" (Take it easy, Mutoi). At one point, while continuing to dance, Mutoi stuck his finger in Pirae's mouth and Pirae whistled to the music while playing the guitar. Monty Python had nothing on these guys. Then Pirae played the spoons, an empty beer bottle, and Mutoi's head. The man was a maestro.

We were invited to a wedding reception in the village. Most of the villagers had been involved in setting up the tent, gathering and cooking the food, and providing the music. The "Maire Nui" canoe team had returned from Hawaii, and the members were given positions of honor at the main table. The meal was wonderful, and the music was even better, lasting well into the next morning with everyone participating in the singing.

During the party, Marc met a young woman named Mareva and was with her constantly until we departed for Tikehau. She wanted Marc to stay with her in her family's valley just east of Tautira.

John and I took our spinning rod to Pirae. He was very gracious in accepting the gift, and I hope he was able to put it to good use. He told us that the weather was right and that we should leave in the morning. On the way back to the boat, we ran into and spoke briefly with the World's Most Beautiful Woman, with whom we had played volleyball while in Bora Bora. Turns out she lived in Tautira and had been visiting family when we met her in Bora Bora.

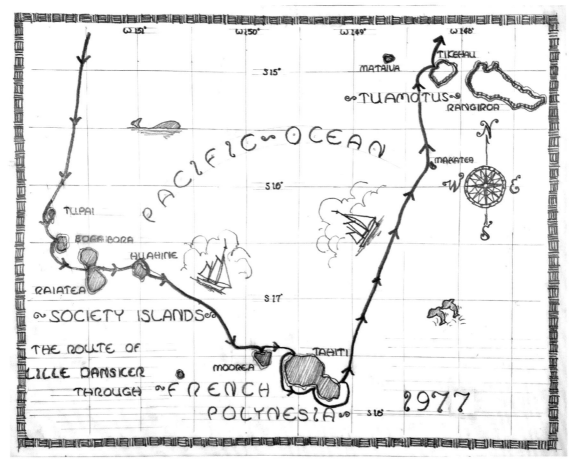

Our route through French Polynesia

17

Sail to Tikehau Atoll

WE DEPARTED for Tikehau the next afternoon, and the wind was perfect, just as Pirae had forecast. Pirae had hauled two huge stalks of bananas out to the boat as gifts for the folks on Tikehau. He explained that growing bananas on some of the atolls was difficult due to the poor soil. We hung the bananas from the mizzen boom gallows.

Marc was very conflicted and had a tough time leaving Mareva. This photo shows him looking back at the valley that could have been his home if he had stayed. I don't know what he was thinking but expect that he might later have had a bit of regret that he left.

The perfect sailing conditions continued all the way to Tikehau. We hooked a large mahi mahi that broke the line and took the lure right before we got him to gaff. Then another one threw the hook. I spent my 0200–0600 watch making some new lures, and then shortly after dawn we caught a 15-pound ono. We had a great

Marc sailing away from Mareva's valley

John with ono

breakfast and enough fish left over for delicious fish sandwiches on baguettes, with good French cheese from the Tautira Chinese store and some fresh lettuce from Pirae's garden.

We bent on the genoa and were making decent speed in perfect conditions. We were abeam Makatea Island at 1730 and sailed close into the lee to take a look. John boated a large tuna as we approached the island. The lee of the island was calm due to the high cliffs, so we dropped sails and drifted while we fried up the tuna for dinner. We were certainly eating well. The waters were alive with fish.

Makatea was uninhabited in 1977 but had been a phosphate mining facility for many years, complete with a village for the families associated with the mining operation. We motored up close to a large steel phosphate loading structure jutting out from the shore. Makatea looked like an interesting place, but there was nowhere to safely anchor that we could see, so we hoisted sail and carried on.

We only had about 40 nautical miles to go, so we carried reduced sail and eased along through the night, staying west of the rhumb line to Tikehau. We didn't want to take any chances with the fickle currents that made the Tuamotus infamous. The moon was in the last quarter and not much help. We sailed with only the main for the last few hours and spotted an island at 0450.

The declination of the sun on November 5 was about 15 degrees south, and the pass at Tikehau was at latitude 15 degrees 00 minutes south, so we had a lot of daylight that day.

When viewing an atoll from offshore, it is difficult to distinguish one atoll from another, as they are very low in profile. We waited until the altitude of the sun was sufficiently high, and then I shot the sun, and the resulting LOP provided reasonable confirmation that the island was Tikehau. The arc of the rising sun aligned with the east–west orientation of the pass, providing additional confirmation. We motored toward the narrow pass on the western flank of the surrounding reef. The location, orientation, and size of the pass confirmed that our navigation was correct.

I know this sounds rather pedantic, but the whole process of confirming Tikehau's identity was very interesting, and that's what the voyage was all about for me. The passage from Tautira to Tikehau for me ranks as one of the all-time great sails. The conditions were perfect, and the voyage went off without a hitch, reinforcing the lessons that local knowledge, prior planning, and waiting for favorable weather almost always pay off.

Tikehau was our first time through an atoll pass. Most authorities recommend transiting a narrow pass into an atoll lagoon at tidal change slack water, but slack-water time can be difficult to calculate and there are conditions that pre-empt slack water. Large ocean swells and/or strong wind-generated waves can overtop the fringing reef, effectively creating a positive head pressure with a higher-than-normal water level within the lagoon. Because most of the water within the lagoon must exit through the pass, there is no slack-water period. In that situation the flow can be a constant and strong ebb.

We were lucky to arrive at the pass when the ocean was relatively calm, and the ebbing current appeared to be only about 2 to 3 knots. We powered partway into the pass to check conditions, then went to neutral and drifted back as we discussed our options. We chose to proceed and maintained enough power to keep the bow dead into the outflowing current. There was a very thin margin for error against the current in the narrowest portion of the channel with breaking surf on either side. Even with those easy conditions, it was a white-knuckles experience.

I think that entering a lagoon at slack water is ideal, but proceeding into a slow

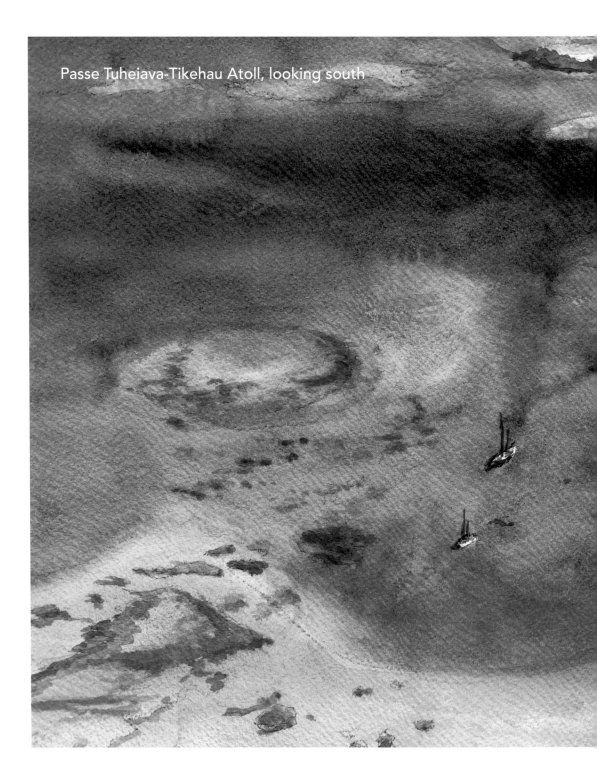

Passe Tuheiava-Tikehau Atoll, looking south

ebbing flow can be a safe approach. The ship's rudder is very effective in those conditions, providing the helmsman with better feel and control. Of course, this assumes that the vessel's engine has sufficient power to overcome the current. Entering during a moderate to strong ebbing tide is not an option if the boat doesn't have an engine. I reckon that sailing vessels can only enter with a favorable wind and at slack or flood water. This is one of those maritime topics that will be forever debated.

Pirae had told us that the Tikehau pass was choked with fish. Sure enough, we hooked a big ono just as we were transiting the narrowest portion of the pass. Of course, right? Catching a fish is almost a certainty if you put a line out in that situation. Marc was quick to gaff the fish and put a wet towel over it in the shade.

As we advanced through the pass, *Lille* started to complain a bit since we had been holding high revs on the engine. The pass gradually opened as we entered the lagoon, and I was able to throttle back some. We resumed breathing. That passage was a bucket-list item.

We saw what looked like a good anchorage just inside and to the north of the channel, and pulled in and dropped in 25 feet. Another boat was anchored nearby.

The other boat was a Tahiti ketch, and Marc said, "Hey, isn't that *Jacques-Louise*, the French boat that we met in Bora Bora?" Once *Lille* was secure, we dove in to cool off and swam over to chat. The owner, Jacques, looked a bit nervous and told us that there were sharks in the cove. We were comfortable being in the water with sharks by then, but soon noticed that there were LOTS of sharks around us. We told Jacques that we would come back in the dinghy, and we then swam back to *Lille*. By the time we were back aboard *Lille*, there were a dozen blacktips right around the boat. That was curious.

It was early morning and we needed to do something with the big ono, so after a brief discussion we decided to sail 7 miles south inside the lagoon to Tuherahera village.

I may have told you already that John is unusually attentive to detail, and as we were hoisting the anchor, he asked, "Hey, did you guys notice that the name *Jacques-Louise* had been painted out and replaced with *Jacques-Gabriel*, and did you also notice that Louise is now built like a brick house?" We weighed anchor and motored over to *Jacques-Louise-Gabriel* to tell Jacques and "Louise" that we would catch up with them in the village.

Our only chart was of the entire northwest portion of the Tuamotus that did not provide any detail of the Tikehau lagoon. Eyeball navigation was mandatory, even if the chart had provided lagoon details. Marc went aloft to guide us through the bommie (patch reef) minefield, and we had a good beam reach easing along at 4–5 knots with no problems.

Immediately after we anchored *Lille* near the concrete wharf at Tuherahera village, several boys in small canoes paddled out and climbed aboard, jabbering and laughing. They wanted us to come ashore, so we inflated *Haze Gray and Underway* and loaded all the boys, the big ono, Pirae's stalks of bananas, Alain's letter of introduction, and our last dozen cans of sardines aboard. With the boys fighting over which ones got to paddle, we meandered our way in—sometimes going backwards, mostly sideways—towing the canoes, and eventually made up to the wharf that was used by the copra schooners.

The village was tiny, and we had no problem finding Alain's grandfather to deliver our letter of introduction, the fish, the bananas, and the sardines. Through a lot of back and forth, we learned that Alain's grandfather had recently turned over chiefly duties to his son (Alain's uncle), hereinafter known as "The Chief."

A runner was sent to notify The Chief, who arrived within minutes accompanied by most of the village inhabitants. Turns out the letter of introduction from Alain was a *Very Big Deal.* Alain had spent many months on Tikehau while growing up and was loved by all and considered to be the shining star of the family and the island. The letter was passed around for everyone to read. We were a bit embarrassed by the unjustified attention, and then The Chief announced *"Promenade, Promenade"* and the crowd echoed *"Promenade, Promenade"*—at which point we were escorted to and loaded aboard a Mazda pickup truck, one of two vehicles in the village. The other vehicle was broken and would otherwise have joined in the promenade.

Alain's grandfather took the seat of honor in the passenger seat in the cab. The Chief, his *vahine*, Marc, John, and I climbed into the truck bed. The helmsman was Felix, The Chief's brother-in-law. We slowly traveled the length of the *motu*, stopping to see the coral stone church and then the coral runway at the airport. Felix turned around and drove back along the coral sand road (there was only one road) to the village, travelling at a speed that allowed all the village boys and dogs to run alongside the truck. Felix constantly honked the horn, and residents who had not joined the throng came out of their houses waving towels. The Chief kept shouting *"Promenade, Promenade,"* and the islanders responded in kind.

The village was sparkling clean and manicured, with white coral walls lining the road, lots of breadfruit trees, and colorful houses full of smiling and happy people. It was even better than I had been imagining all those years of reading books about the Tuamotus by Charles Nordoff, James Norman Hall, and William Albert Robinson.

We had dinner with Felix, The Chief, Alain's other uncle Roland, and Roland's *vahine* Titina. Felix prepared the ono in a coconut milk base—hands-down the best fish I have ever tasted.

We told The Chief that there was another boat anchored near the pass, and he said that made a total of six boats that had visited Tikihau in 1977.

Alain's grandfather stopped by after dinner for coffee and explained that he appreciated our efforts to speak his language and he also appreciated that we didn't wear bikini shorts like the Frenchmen. You just never know what is going to resonate. You might think that I am being unfair towards the French, but let me tell you—I consider the French to be up there with the Kiwis when it comes to sailing prowess. After all, they have won just about every singlehanded and team round-the-world race, while wearing only hot pink bikini foulweather gear, and have established all kinds of sailing speed records while wearing the same gear. Those guys are nuts about sailing and have my utmost admiration for their sailing abilities, regardless of their sailing livery.

Vincent and Clay

18

Motu Adventures

FELIX ASKED US to take him and his two sons to his bungalow on Motu Tematuopapahia, 12 miles north across the lagoon. We got an early start the next day. The wind was 10–15 out of the east. There were fewer bommies in the middle portion of the lagoon, but Marc stayed aloft, coming down once or twice to refresh himself by dumping a bucket of seawater over his head. The sun was brutal.

The anchorage within the lagoon at Motu Tematuopapahia was on a bit of a lee shore, but the weather was stable and showing only soft trade wind clouds. We set two anchors in a sand bottom and went ashore. The *motu*, about 15 kilometers long by 0.5 kilometer wide, was completely covered with coconut palms. Felix's was one of many properties on the *motu*, and while most had a small garden and simple living quarters, copra harvesting was the main endeavor. Like Felix, most of the owners lived in Tuherehera village and came to the *motu* as needed to care for their copra plantations.

We spent the next few days helping Felix tend his copra, spearfishing on the outside reef, visiting his neighbors on the *motu*. We ate healthy meals that included fish, octopus, lobster, and numerous dishes made from the coconut palm (*Cocos nucifera*), including my favorite, heart of palm in coconut milk. Felix always kept a stash of *ipo*, a sugary white-flour pastry boiled in water. His twin sons Victor and Vincent were three years old at the time, and I never saw them without their faces smeared with flour and a partially eaten *ipo* in their tiny hands.

With the sun directly over our latitude, the days were long and hot, and we were constantly cutting open green coconuts to drink the coconut water and then eat the soft spoon meat using a spoon cut and shaped from the hull of the coconut.

Coconut milk differs from coconut water. The milk is made from mature (brown) coconuts by scraping out the hard meat with a serrated tool and then squeezing and straining the meat through cheesecloth. Adding water thins the milk, and there are infinite grades of coconut milk. Most meals prepared in the Tuamotus in those days included at least one dish made with coconut milk.

Commercial-scale copra harvesting started in the 19th century and was still going strong on Tikehau in 1977. Copra is the dried meat or kernel of the mature brown coconut. Felix and his neighboring farmers gathered the brown coconuts, removed the husk, cracked the nut in half, and then set the halves white-side up on racks in the sun to desiccate. After sufficient drying, the meat was removed from the shell, loaded into burlap bags, and hauled back to Tuherahera village in various boats. A fleet of copra schooners made regular runs among the various atolls of the Tuamotu Archipelago to offload goods for the islanders and then onload the bags of copra for transport back to Papeete.

The copra was eventually processed by crushing the dried meat to yield 70 percent coconut oil and 30 percent coconut cake (animal feed). Coconut oil has multiple uses. It is used as the base ingredient in many soaps, cosmetics, and pharmaceuticals. Coconut-oil bar soap lathers in seawater, making it very useful on a voyaging sailboat. We had purchased a few bars of coconut-oil soap from the Chinese store in Papeete, and that made seawater baths on deck much better. We should have purchased more bars.

Felix had an old beater car that we had to push-start. Marc adjusted the carburetor, and we drove several kilometers down the trail that wound amongst the palm trees. A friend from the village had asked Felix to feed his pigs. The pigs' diet consisted of coconut, land crabs, and whatever they could scrounge from the beach. The five pigs must have recognized the sound of Felix's car and came running to greet us. Felix introduced us to each pig by name. I only remember that one was named Hamilton, which was easy for me to remember because that was my father's name.

During the drive back to his bungalow, Felix pointed out the various stages of coconut palm growth. Like most things in nature, the subject was a lot more involved than might be expected. Felix's knowledge of the process had been handed down through generations, and it appeared to me that he had achieved near perfection. Of course, only nature can achieve perfection.

Our first spearfishing dive on the outside reef near Felix's house was otherworldly. Felix gave us some brief instructions about getting in and out of the surf and which fish to shoot. We had to time the swell, dive in between wave sets, and then go like hell to get away from the razor-sharp coral reef before the next wave consumed us.

I may never see a healthier reef system. It was like being inside an aquarium. The water was crystal clear once we got away from air-entrained water in the surf zone close to the reef. The vibrant-colored reef dropped off steeply into the deep blue.

Blacktip shark

We had to push fish out of the way to get a good shot at the fish we wanted. Large grouper were everywhere, but Felix told us they were *aita maitai*, and we assumed that he was referring to ciguatera poisoning.

I had given my *pupue* (speargun) to Felix and was using a pathetic little aluminum double arbalete gun about 3 feet long that I brought from Hawaii. Felix insisted on holding the fish stringer, and we soon had enough good fish on the stringer. The blacktip sharks had been gathering around us, and then a couple of pesky whitetips joined in. We had learned that whitetips could be ornery and unpredictable. The blacktips are gorgeous animals, a close second to oceanic blues. There were more than 100 sharks in the immediate vicinity, including blacktips, whitetips, and some grays. The situation was getting dicey. John had become separated from the rest of us and was in the surf zone with poor visibility. One of the whitetips began to act agitated and charged at John several times, becoming more and more aggressive with each charge. John tried to fend off the shark by pushing his speargun into the gut of the shark, with little effect. John thought the next charge might be the real thing. Before the shark could circle back, a wave lifted John and tossed him ass-over-teakettle onto the exposed reef.

Marc and I were with Felix when another whitetip became a bit too interested in the stringer of fish that Felix was protecting, and we had to jab at him with our *pupue*. Felix would press the stringer to his chest and turn his back to the shark. Felix signaled for us to move to the shore, but as we got close to the reef face, the whitetip did something I had never seen. He hunched his back and rolled his eyes back into the sockets, showing only the white of his eyes and then went in hard for the fish stringer in a berserk manner. We were all jabbing at him, and he chomped down on my speargun, breaking it in half. No big loss, but that guy was seriously pissed off. But so was Felix, who then speared the shark right in the head. Felix retrieved his barbless spear, and the other sharks had the injured shark reduced to nothing in short order.

We had lingered too long in the break zone and sure enough, a large wave rolled Marc and me onto the reef and deposited us right next to John in a pile of bodies. I don't know how Felix avoided the same fate, but he casually climbed out, looked down at us, and had a good long laugh. He had saved the fish stringer. Luckily, we only had minor scrapes and cuts and had learned that a good wash with hydrogen peroxide followed by a dab of Neosporin would help prevent infection—maybe.

Back at the bungalow, Felix and John prepared the *himaa* and cooked the fish. During the meal, John told us that his episode with the shark was the scariest thing he had ever experienced. I concurred. No comment from Marc. Felix admitted that it was an adventure but then explained that he did not like having to spear the shark because sharks were his friends. He shot the shark because he felt responsible for our safety. We all agreed that we were thankful for the experience but happy to be done with the sharks for the day.

Felix told us how young Tuamotuan children are taught to co-exist with sharks. A shallow hole is dug in the sand at the edge of the lagoon and flooded with seawater. Captured baby blacktips are put into the small pool, and the kids follow into the pool and learn to maneuver with and gently but firmly fend off the sharks, both species gradually becoming comfortable with the arrangement. The islanders' existence is dependent on being in the water, and they must learn to share the environment with the natural inhabitants and thus become natural inhabitants themselves.

We were famished and started with a big bowl of *poisson cru* and then some heart of palm in coconut milk. With all the recent exercise and healthy food, we

Felix and John cooking fish

were getting back into shape and feeling good after our period of decadent living in Papeete.

After we completed our copra chores, the next day Felix took us to the shipwreck site of the three-masted schooner *Valrosa*. The surf was higher than the day before and we debated proceeding but finally dove in, to find ourselves in an underwater graveyard of bronze ship fittings, two large engines, and an intact lead keel, all surrounded by thousands of huge fish.

We didn't carry spearguns because Felix had explained earlier that the fish near the wreck were *aita maitai*, and we assumed that perhaps the huge chunk of lead was the culprit. I got some rough measurements of the keel and later calculated that it weighed about 40 tons. We found bronze portholes, cleats, hawsepipes, a gigantic windlass, and lots of other miscellaneous hardware. We took nothing, and just gazed in awe. It was a spooky place, best left alone. The sharks were there, but not interested in us.

The shattered hull of *Valrosa* was far down the very steep slope of the reef, resting on a sand ledge in about 100 feet of water. I imagined that the ship had crashed headlong into the reef, dislodging the keel, then slowly broken apart over time to eventually drop off the edge into the deep. A stump of the foremast remained.

I noticed Marc effortlessly kicking his way down to the wreck, accompanied by a huge black ulua (jack crevally). I followed and made it to the broken tip of the foremast stump. Marc continued to the foredeck. The ulua stayed with us back to the surface before slowly wandering away. I assumed that the ulua was the "Guardian" and was just asserting his territorial authority. We later named him "The Big Kahuna."

We dove on the wreck debris field for a couple of hours because it was so incredible and strange. "The Big Kahuna" made close passes now and then and seemed to be getting annoyed with our presence, so we decided to get out of the water. John got rolled by a wave after he had climbed out and lost his prescription-lens diving mask, which was sucked back into the water by the return flow. Marc and I looked for it with no luck, and then Marc got rolled when he exited, cutting his legs and back and shredding his swimsuit. We were experiencing some tough lessons, but all agreed that it was the coolest skin-diving we had ever done.

I have since been diving on countless reefs in the Pacific, including the wonderful underwater coral gardens of Fulaga Island in the Lau group, Fiji, and the lush, apex-predator-dominated reefs of Palmyra Atoll, but Tikehau still ranks as my favorite.

The areas where we dove were on the exposed coast of Tikehau, so the reef didn't have the delicate corals of more protected reefs. Rather, the multicolored corals were bold and massive, and the steep drop-off into the dark abyss was spectacular and somewhat frightening. We were privileged to have the opportunity to visit the Tikehau reefs, and I noted that Felix displayed a quiet reverence as we prepared for the dives. I felt that we had entered a sanctuary.

Marc and Clay with Felix and his sons and neighbors

John and Felix during motor-sail back to the village

The dives of the last two days reinforced my appreciation for the undersea environment, realizing that we were uninvited visitors in an alien world. But, I also knew that if we could abide the laws of nature and enter the environment with an open mind, we could thrive and perhaps become welcomed guests. We would never have the Polynesian understanding of the natural world, an understanding that has evolved over thousands of years, but the dives with Felix were humbling experiences and we were better participants for it.

Felix and his sons came to dinner on the boat that night, and Felix brought his accordion. He played a kind of reggae that he had learned from his grandfather, who was from Martinique.

We made another run down the *motu* to feed Hamilton and his brethren. They were happy to see us, and we talked for a while. During the drive back we stopped and gathered a load of green drinking coconuts. We then hurried to sweep out the bungalow, loaded several burlap bags of copra aboard *Lille*, weighed anchors, and departed for Tuherahera village.

Felix navigated us to one of Roland's fish traps. Roland was a successful businessman, maintaining several fish traps within the lagoon, and he regularly shipped fish to Papeete aboard the copra schooners. Felix wanted to gather pahua, which proliferated around the fish trap for some reason. In short order we had filled a burlap bag full of pahua. We shared a bowl of pahua in coconut milk as we completed the sail to the village. We sent Marc's portion aloft in a coconut shell cup.

We had dinner at Roland's house that night. Felix prepared a delicious sautéed pahua dish accompanied by baked parrotfish and a heart of palm salad with papaya seed dressing. The man could have been a chef in Paris. Roland talked at length about his fish business. His fish traps required constant maintenance, and the sometimes unscheduled arrival of a copra schooner meant that he had to scramble to harvest the fish from the traps in a very short period in order to get the product loaded in time for the schooner departure. Alain was his business liaison in Papeete and kept the business sound and viable.

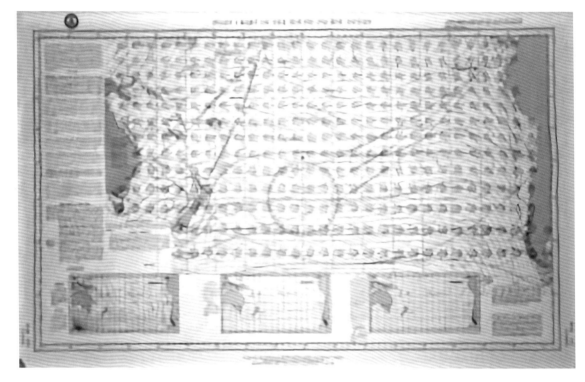

South Pacific pilot chart for November

19

Back to the Blue

JACQUES-GABRIEL ARRIVED in the village anchorage the next morning, and Jacques came aboard for a chat. He told us that their sail from Papeete had taken six days in terrible headwinds. I said a silent thank-you to Pirae for his insistence that we wait in Tautira until the winds became more favorable. Then Jacques told us that just prior to leaving Papeete he had found a new first mate and he had always made a practice of changing the boat name to include that of the new mate. But he had done a half-assed rush job (that is not the expression he used) of painting the new name to reflect the upgrade. We all, including Jacques, placed bets on how many times the boat name would change before arriving back in France. I did not follow up; therefore, the results of the bet are inconclusive.

The Chief announced another Promenade in honor of Jacques and Gabriel—so, clad in bikinis, they were loaded aboard the Mazda with Alain's grandfather and The Chief. Felix manned the helm. Marc had helped to get the other vehicle running, sort of, and we boarded that one, with a fellow named Cocoio at the helm. Cocoio was from Mataiva, the atoll 20 nautical miles northwest of Tikehau, and was on Tikehau working copra. "Return of Promenade" was a big success, and Jacques made a very humble and heartfelt thank-you speech afterwards. At least I think it was humble and heartfelt. He spoke French, so actually I have no idea what he said.

Felix and Roland shuttled a crowd of about 25 folks out to the boat the next day for a visit. The postwoman was in the group and brought a packet of letters for us. That was a real pleasant surprise. Apparently, Chief Inspector Clouseau had asked the postmaster in the Papeete Bureau de Poste to forward our mail to Tikehau.

Cocoio was also in the group and asked a lot of good questions about the boat. He then asked if we knew the fellows on *Hokulea* and got a bit emotional as he told about the canoe's visit to Mataiva the previous year. He wanted to go on a canoe voyage someday. Cocoio was a good man, and I hope he was able to realize his dream. He later harvested about 40 green coconuts for us to drink during the voyage home to Hawaii.

We got ready to leave on Sunday for Hawaii, but the wind was very light and Felix told us it would remain so for a few more days.

Roland asked us to go with him to the evening church service, and we joined what appeared to be the entire population of the village. There was a lot of beautiful singing, which, from my experience is common to most churches throughout the Pacific islands. After each song The Chief would stand up in front and ask a question about Noah's Ark, the topic for that evening's sermon. Anyone was permitted to answer, and some of the answers rambled on for several minutes, during which one middle-aged fellow towards the back would stand and start singing a hymn in a very loud voice. Fortunately, he had a beautiful tenor singing voice and no one in the congregation objected. The person answering The Chief's question just continued answering, a bit louder but uninterrupted.

We sat next to Roland's *vahine*, Titina, who spoke English, and she helped translate because our Tahitian language education had not yet included Biblical passages. During this segment of the service, an elderly woman sitting in the pew behind us kept tapping us on the back and asking us if we were Russians and did we have any more cans of sardines. Each time, Titina would turn around and patiently say to the elderly woman, "*Haere maru, haere maru.*"

At one point The Chief asked, "How long did it rain in the story of Noah's Ark?" Someone would stand and talk for several minutes and then sit down, hopeful that the answer was correct. The Chief would then respond, "*Aita*" (No). This went on for about an hour with The Chief responding "*Aita*" to each answer. A young man up front answered, "601½ years." The tenor stopped singing, the room went quiet, we leaned forward in our pews. The Chief hesitated, rubbed his chin, and eventully said, "*Aita.*" John sat back and let out a groan, and the attempts to answer the Noah's Ark question resumed.

After a few more incorrect answers, John leaned forward, got the attention of the man in front of us, and whispered (with Titina's translation assistance), "PLEASE tell The Chief that it rained for 40 days and 40 nights." We were hopeful that John had solved the puzzle, but something must have been lost in translation and that didn't work. Finally, Titina patted John on the knee, gave him a wink, and stood up. After The Chief acknowledged that Titina had the floor, Titina said, "It rained for 40 days and 40 nights." The Chief smiled and nodded his head, to the immense satisfaction and admiration of the congregation.

The Tahitian Pavarotti, joined by the entire congregation, broke into a rousing chorus of "I Sing a Song of the Saints of God." I got chicken skin hearing that beautiful melody. Raising both hands high, I praised the Lord that the Q&A was done.

The service lasted three hours and 45 minutes and was followed by donuts and coffee. One guy put sardines on his donut. As we were leaving, most members of the congregation congratulated Titina for knowing and providing the correct answer.

During the next couple of days we sanded and painted the green topsides and put a coat of spar varnish on the rails so that *Lille* would feel proud for the voyage home. The weather improved and we made final preparations to leave. Saying goodbye was difficult. Our time in Tikehau had been the highlight of the voyage for me. We had worked, played, and communed with happy people, whose kindness and goodness were genuine and absolute. We moved *Lille* to the dock and topped off the water tanks. We gave Felix another one of the spearguns, a spool of nylon line, and a few cans of Dinty Moore beef stew. He gave us 5 gallons of diesel (all he had) and some great memories. Villagers wandered down to the dock and placed shell *lei* around our necks. We presented our Hawaii flag to The Chief and threw off the lines at 1445. Marc yelled out "*Promenade, Promenade, Aloha,*" to which everyone laughed and yelled back "*Promenade, Promenade, Bon Voyage.*" Too much!!

Sailing across the lagoon was easy. The flow in the pass was ebbing, and *Lille* flew out into the blue. Marc remained aloft as we rocketed out of the pass, later saying it had been an E Ticket Ride. We settled down and focused on helping *Lille* take us home.

In the days leading up to departure from Tikehau, I spent considerable time studying the November pilot charts of the South Pacific and the December pilot charts of the North Pacific. While historical data showed less than ideal conditions for a voyage to Hawaii, the charts gave us reasonable assurance of manageable winds.

Pilot charts provide an abundance of historical information founded upon the research conducted by Lt. Matthew Fontaine Maury, USN in the early 19th century. Matthew Maury was an astronomer, oceanographer, meteorologist, cartographer, and geologist and became known as the "Scientist of the Seas."

I can spend hours examining nautical charts and pilot charts, and am always amazed at the wealth of information that can be gleaned from detailed study. For me, studying a nautical chart is like reading a good book. The earliest charts of the Pacific provided very rudimentary data, but were incredibly accurate, considering the limited resources available at the time. Charts have improved over the

PILOT CHART DATA FOR NOVEMBER 10 DEGREES SOUTH TO EQUATOR		
Wind Direction	Wind Force (Beaufort Scale)	% of Time from Direction
North	4	15
Northeast	3	15
East	4	50
Southeast	4	10
South	3	10
Southwest	NA	0
West	NA	0
Northwest	NA	0

PILOT CHART DATA FOR DECEMBER EQUATOR TO 10 DEGREES NORTH		
Wind Direction	Wind Force (Beaufort Scale)	% of Time from Direction
North	3	5
Northeast	4	10
East	4	45
Southeast	4	35
South	3	0–2
Southwest	1	0–1
West	2	0–2
Northwest	NA	0

Pilot Chart data for November, 10 degrees south to the Equator
Pilot Chart data for December, Equator to 10 degrees north

years and the amount of information contained in them has increased substantially. Hydrographic surveys by the major maritime countries are constantly updating the important data and thus making piloting and navigation more accurate and safer.

When preparing for our voyage, I had brought pilot charts along with nautical charts knowing that the historical conditions provided by pilot charts during the relevant months could provide information about wind direction and speed, currents, surface pressure, air and sea temperature, tropical cyclones, wave heights, magnetic variation, visibility, great circle sailing routes, and average percentage of gales. A wind rose full of good information is shown for each 5-degree block of a pilot chart.

The South Pacific pilot chart showed the above data along our planned route in the area from 10 degrees south to the equator.

While we would have preferred to start out with southeast trades, history favored easterly and perhaps some northeasterly quadrant winds. I planned to cross the equator at 145 degrees west in hopes of experiencing reaching conditions when we picked up the northeast trades. And of course there were the unknowns associated with our old friend the ITCZ, so every bit of easting would help.

The North Pacific pilot chart showed the above data along our planned route in the area from the equator to 10 degrees north. The data looked promising, but I didn't trust it since that area was basically all within the ITCZ. We kept our fingers crossed that history would hold and Mother would treat us kindly.

				BEAUFORT SCALE	
Beaufort Number	Name	Knots	MPH	Effects Observed Far From Land	Effects Observed On Land
0	Calm	Under 1	Under 1	Sea like mirror.	Calm; smoke rises vertically
1	Light Air	1-3	1-3	Ripples with appearances of scales; no foam crests.	Direction of wind shown by smoke drift, but not by wind vanes.
2	Light Breeze	4-6	4-7	Small wavelets; crests of glassy appearance, not breaking.	Wind felt on face; leaves rustle; ordinary vane moved by wind.
3	Gentle Breeze	7-10	8-12	Large wavelets; crests begin to break; scattered whitecaps.	Leaves and small twigs in constant motion; wind extends light flag.
4	Moderate Breeze	11-16	13-18	Small waves, becoming longer; numerous whitecaps.	Raises dust and loose paper, small branches are moved.
5	Fresh Breeze	17-21	19-24	Moderate waves, taking longer form; many whitecaps; some spray.	Small trees in leaf begin to sway; crested wavelets form on inland waters.
6	Strong Breeze	22-27	25-31	Larger waves forming; whitecaps everywhere; more spray.	Large branches in motion; whistling heard in telegraph wires; umbrellas used with difficulty.
7	Near Gale	28-33	32-38	Sea heaps up; white foam from breakinig waves begins to be blown in streaks.	Whole trees in motion; inconvenience felt in walking against the wind.
8	Gale	34-40	39-46	Moderately high waves of greater length; edges of crests begin to break into spindrift; foam is blown in well-marked streaks.	Breaks twigs off trees; generally impedes progress.
9	Strong Gale	41-47	47-54	High waves; sea begins to roll; dense streaks of foam; spray may reduce visibility.	Slight structural damage occurs (chimney pots and slate removed).
10	Storm	48-55	55-63	Very high waves with overhanging crests; sea takes white appearance as foam is blown in very dense streaks; rolling is heavy and visibility reduced.	Seldom experienced inland; trees uprooted; considerable structural damage occurs.
11	Violent Storm	56-63	64-72	Exceptionally high waves; sea covered with white foam patches; visibility still more reduced.	Very rarely experienced; accompanied by widespread damage.
12	Hurricane	64 and over	73 and over	Air filled with foam; sea completely white with driving spray; visibility reduced.	

Beaufort Scale

We had light easterly winds for the first couple of days, sailing full and by, and were making decent progress, catching fish, tackling various cleaning/organizing projects, and enjoying being back out in the Big Blue.

While we were in Tautira, Pirae had traded some of his small duster fishing lures for some of our big ahi lures. He said that ono liked the dusters and he wanted to go after some big ahi. The trade worked out well for us. I hope Pirae caught some giant ahi. The dusters didn't get torn up by ono strikes like the plastic skirts. Ono have very pronounced and sharp teeth, and we sometimes had to replace plastic skirts after only a couple of ono hits.

Marc caught a small ono early Thanksgiving morning, and we prepared a mid-afternoon feast. We steamed the fish over onions with oregano, bay leaf, and cream sauce.

In an attempt at a bit of tradition, we also pulled out a can of "Whole Chicken" as a substitute for whole turkey, which would have required an exceptionally large can. Opening a can of whole chicken is a risky business. One must choose which end to open in hopes of first revealing the forward end of the bird. If one chooses incorrectly, the initial shock can be an appetite suppressant.

Having experienced opening the wrong end earlier in the voyage, we sat in the cockpit, befuddled and hesitant to open the can. We discussed the matter at length and wondered why whole-chicken canning companies do not standardize the labeling of the whole-chicken orientation within the can. The conclusion was that someone (the labeling foreman?) on the canning assembly line took sadistic pleasure in the random orientation. We agreed to a best-two-out-of-three coin toss to determine which end to open, and we also agreed to a Janken Po (Japanese Rock, Paper, Scissors) to determine which one of us would open the can. John and I then learned that fearlessness does in fact have limits when Marc said he just could not do it and asked that he be excused from the selection proceedings. I lost the Janken Po and then nervously opened the can with shaking hands but singular purpose. I noticed that Marc could not watch. *Hallelujah!!* Although my nervousness caused me to spill most of the canned chicken juice on my lap, we got lucky with the orientation and were able to then cook the canned whole chicken and sort of enjoy the meal.

During the Thanksgiving meal John suggested that we each state a few of our favorite toasts, sayings, and/or life lessons. This session lasted well into the afternoon, and some of the memorable ones included:

Indo-Pacific gecko (*Hemidactylus garnotii*)

"Enough is as good as a feast"

"Too much is not enough"

"I Feel like letting my freak flag fly"

"Mujeres sin pantalones"

"Hunger is the best sauce"

"You shouldn't let other people get your kicks for you"

"At least there's one good thing about it"

"A hand in the bush is one hell of lot better than two birds"

"A place for everything and everything all over the place"

"Indecision is the key to flexibility"

"God tempers the wind to the shorn lamb"

"Hallelujah, Hallelujah, Hallelujah"

"Just one look, I was a bad mess"

"Meet the new boss, same as the old boss"

We had picked up a stowaway gecko in Tikehau (or perhaps back in Tahiti) and he came into the cockpit for some fresh air, sunshine, and a bit of exercise each afternoon, usually during the first dog watch. We never figured out where he bunked or why he hadn't offered to stand a night watch. We reckoned he was just a pleasant freeloader looking for a bit of adventure, and we named him Wally.

Wally showed up early on Thanksgiving Day as we were having our discussion about canned whole chicken, and the conversation appeared to make him nervous but interested, nonetheless. He was probably thinking, "The boys back home will never believe this shit."

Most gecko species have adhesive spatula-shaped foot pads that adhere to surfaces by electrostatic interaction caused by contact electrification. This enabled Wally to walk upside down in his perambulations around the boat. But while foot adhesion increases with humidity, adhesion is reduced in total immersion. That was apparently Wally's demise when he made his appearance one afternoon later in the voyage during rough conditions. Sliding down a big swell, *Lille* buried her bow and water flowed down the deck and washed the poor bugger out of a deck scupper. Marc was on it and immediately sang out, "Gecko overboard" and kept his eyes on the spot where he had last seen Wally. Alas, our recovery efforts were futile, and we lost Wally. I remain hopeful that he was able to find a comfortable piece of flotsam and eventually make it ashore somewhere.

The moon was full on November 25 and waning gibbous on the 27th. Marc had the second dog watch, during which he yelled down to me, "It's big and it's there." That was an unusual wake-up call, and I bounded on deck to see Marc pointing off to starboard at a huge light that appeared that it would very soon overwhelm us. We then simultaneously realized that it was the rising moon and not a ship. That was amazing. It just shows how a sleep-deprived watch-stander's mind can create havoc.

During my 0200–0600 watch, we were easing along in pleasant conditions, and I suddenly felt as though *Lille* had departed the surface of the ocean and we were sailing to the moon. I am almost certain that we were not actually sailing to the moon, but just accepted it and even though I was a bit concerned about our provisions, felt good about a much longer voyage. *Sailing Somewhere Cosmic.* I was proud of *Lille* for taking the scenic route. I don't recall how long that lasted but it was indeed fun, and we eventually landed back in the ocean and resumed our lot as Earthbound misfits.

We were slowly working our way north towards home when the wind backed to the north, and we tacked over to port to gain some easting. We decided that if the north wind persisted, visiting the Marquesas might be a good unplanned diversion. *Sailing Somewhere East.* The wind was initially 10–15 and pleasant but increased to 20–25 with a large accompanying sea. We were back into wet conditions but were making progress towards the Marquesas.

Marc with ono

We slogged our way to within about 100 miles of Nuku Hiva when the wind gradually clocked to the east at 30 knots. Done deal. Neither *Lille* nor we were up for the windward plunge to the Marquesas. Mother was just messing with us, so, abiding her rather confounding sense of humor, we tacked back over to starboard and headed home, reefed down in good reaching conditions.

Homeward bound

20

Homeward Bound

WE GOT INTO A GOOD daily-chores routine: I performed engine checks and cleaned the engine room; Marc cleaned the galley and 'midship cabin; John cleaned the main cabin and the doghouse. As always, we each performed regular rigging checks while on watch. We had learned from experience that good housekeeping can help lead to a safe ship, and that results in sounder sleep and a happier crew, so we made our bunks and squared away our personal kit each day. The routine was valuable and helped maintain our focus. Perhaps we were each neat freaks anyway. Whatever.

At 8 degrees south the wind eased a bit, and we were able to open the hatches, air out the cabins, and bring the bedding topside to dry in the sunshine. *Lille* was feeling good. We caught a 20-pound ono and John made a great dinner that included hush puppies, somehow made using our last box of Snackin' Cake mixed with some diced onion and a touch of Zatarain's Crab Boil. We ate dinner in the cockpit, and just before sunset a huge pod of pilot whales surfaced on the port side. For some reason it seemed that sea life always joined us on the port side… We got ready to jump in and hang on a line, but we were sailing too fast and realized that it would be embarrassing if all three of us went adrift as *Lille* sailed home alone. She was smelling the barn and didn't want to slow down. The pilot whales stayed with us for about an hour. Life was indeed good!

I had long planned to read James Michener's *Hawaii* during the voyage home and had gotten to the chapter in which the captain of the Tahitian sailing canoe was concerned about making his easting on the voyage to Hawaii. That was meaningful and I could certainly relate. The Polynesians sailed close to the wind until they reached the guide star for the Big Island. That star was and is Hokule'a (Arcturus). Hokule'a has a declination of approximately 19 degrees 10 minutes north, roughly the same latitude as the southernmost portion of the Big Island. When the wayfinder noted that Hokule'a was directly overhead, he was confident that he could turn the canoe downwind (in prevailing trade winds) and find the Big Island.

Except for one day with light conditions, the wind held steady from the northeast at 15–20 and we crossed the equator in 146 degrees west longitude. It was a very busy day. There was a big northeasterly swell running, so we had to crack off a bit to keep from pounding, but the ocean was alive. We decided to give two of the large lures a go, one on a handline and the other on the Penn Senator. Almost immediately we got a double hook-up but lost both lures and the attached fishes.

We didn't see the fish on the handline before it broke the leader, but it must have been massive. It was fortunate that we lost it. But the fish on the Senator was a real nice mahi that we lost right up close to the stern. We reckoned the leader was just worn out by prior ono hits. We rigged a new leader and a duster to the Senator and soon caught a smallish mahi for dinner.

We had been saving a bottle of champagne that Uncle Odie had given us, so we spliced the main brace and shared the champagne at dinner. We toasted Odie, Ah-Ki, Teraii, Alain, Alex, Marcel, the basketball team, the World's Most Beautiful Woman, Temanu, Darlene, Rodo, Tina, Chief Inspector Clouseau, Pirae, Mutoi, Mareva, Jacques Cousteau, Mau Piailug, James Cook, William Bligh, Sir Joseph Banks, Charles Darwin, Felix, Roland, The Chief, Alain's grandfather, the Tahitian Pavarotti, Titina, Jacques, ~~Louise~~-Gabriel, Cocoio, Matthew Maury, Chester Nimitz, and most importantly Mother Ocean, by which point we had drained the bottle. The sunset was amazing with orange and blue stripes. It may have been the champagne. We were *LIVING LARGE,* but, as always, the conversation eventually drifted to the subject of women and more specifically the lack thereof. We were ready to get home.

We had decent wind direction and speed for a couple of days after the equator crossing, but we got into gale conditions beginning in 5 degrees north latitude and started having gear failures. That wasn't so bad because it kept us busy making repairs. The bobstay parted at the stem fitting, which required that John lie down facing aft in the safety netting slung beneath the bowsprit in order to shackle in a length of ⅜-inch chain and a turnbuckle. That worked out well, because he also checked off his afternoon bath at the same time with the constant dunkings. I guess that was what is now referred to as multitasking. The mizzen starboard running backstay parted at the mast fitting, and Marc went aloft to make the repair. (He enjoyed being up there and sometimes went aloft just for the hell of it.) Those runners sure gave us fits. It might have been that we just didn't have the rig properly tuned and kept snap-loading the runners. A couple of piston hanks on the jib let go and the reef cringle on the leech of the jib blew out. Our sewing skills had improved, and we got the jib repaired and hoisted again within a couple of hours.

We were in and out of squalls and counted seven in one hour. Back in the ITCZ, with all its natural chaos—what a place! Fortunately, the wind direction was good. We did take a bit of a knockdown during a very heavy sudden squall one morning about 0600. We only had up the reefed jib and double-reefed main and managed to douse quickly and then get squared away. And we were able to top off our water tanks with delicious rainwater. Once again, the ITCZ was proving to be an interesting tourist attraction, but we were hoping for an abbreviated visit this time. I had to carry a DR plot for three days without a celestial fix due to the constant rain and overcast.

We sailed into "The Void" at 8 degrees north latitude and once again entered The Silent World. Absolutely no sound—nothing. During my night watch I brought the RDF topside and tuned into KPOI and heard "Go Your Own Way" by Fleetwood Mac. I cranked it up and John and Marc joined me. It was amazing to be in a world without sound and to have that song defining the world. We needed to have some gigantic speakers on deck at full volume to fully appreciate the music but had to make do with what the RDF provided.

I have since imagined a trip back to the ITCZ for the purpose of finding The Void and just hanging out and listening to music. I think the oceanic inhabitants would appreciate the new dimension. "On the Turning Away" by Pink Floyd would be an appropriate song. David Gilmour's guitar solo would be perfect for the situation. I picture a full-moon night and diving down to about 40 feet to look back up at *Lille* with that song transmitting through the hull to fill the void. The fish, dolphins, and whales are gathered close by to feel the bass. Returning to the surface and climbing aboard, I see my old friend Orion is making his way to the zenith as the music reaches the crescendo. Life is pretty good…

The sun came out when we reached 10 north, where we then had 20–25 knots of east-northeast wind and long period swells of 15–20 feet. Magnificent sailing! The best of the entire trip. Well, maybe second only to the voyage from Tautira to Tikehau. *Lille* was loving it. The tops of the waves were being blown off and the spray reached the top of the mast. A wave broke over the partially open companionway hatch and douched the stove, so we went without hot food for a couple of days. It felt kind of nostalgic, having to do battle with that bitch of a stove again. On the second day, I found myself opening a can of Van Camps pork and beans and eating

Lille "Running large before the north-east trade winds"

right out of the can. John admitted that he had just finished a can of cold corned beef hash. What a life! Hoo-yah.

The frequency of the squalls diminished as we left the ITCZ, and we made consistently good daily runs. When we got the stove working again, we put out a line and boated a 15-pound mahi. That was a much-needed hot meal.

We found that sailing in schooner configuration with jib, double-reef main, and single-reefed mizzen balanced the boat well in 25-knot northeast-wind reaching conditions. We caught a small mahi and a 30-pound ono at 15 north and had some great meals.

The wind clocked to east for a day, and we were able to broad-reach under genoa, full main, and single-reefed mizzen, making the best boat speed of the voyage. Even though we were a bit overpowered, *Lille* was built for those conditions and was loving it. As Richard Henry Dana put it in *Two Years Before the Mast*, we were "Running large before the north-east trade winds."

During the last few months, we had become decent sailors and were able to help *Lille* find her rhythm. By that I mean that the boat was balanced for the wind and sea conditions and moving efficiently. That rhythm is one thing that I like about sailing. It is the ultimate relative-motion problem. The boat and everything else are moving. The ocean and her inhabitants are moving, the atmosphere is moving, the Earth is turning, and the celestial bodies are moving. Our muscles are constantly moving, even while we are sleeping as we subconsciously work to remain in our bunks. Finding a comfortable rhythm is a key component of voyaging. It becomes a sort of Zen thing when done well. The secret is to "allow" the boat to sail to her potential. But, finding that rhythm can be a challenge.

Most new sailors tend to over-trim and over-steer, as we did earlier in the voyage. After learning to trim the sails so that they breathe and letting *Lille* find the sweet spot, we minimized steering. It is equivalent to giving a horse free rein. Over-steering makes the boat wander, adds miles, and is slow. The rudder is essentially a brake as it creates drag when turned. When sailing upwind, sailboat drivers are constantly searching for the "groove," a situation in time and space when the sails are properly trimmed, the rudder is balanced, and weight distribution is correct. The boat settles into optimum speed and performance with minimum course wandering. When the groove is attained, the boat is doing her best. The helmsman can feel the boat take off as soon as he has found the groove. It is a marvelous feeling. Once attained, the goal is to keep the boat "in the groove." I don't know if the expression was originally a sailing term or a jazz term, but it fits sailing perfectly.

We got into gale conditions again for about a day, took in some deep reefs, and kept moving. The forecast on WWVH (the National Institute of Standards transmitter out of Kekaha, Kauai) informed us that gale warnings were posted for all Hawaiian waters. But somehow, the winter solstice, December 21, was a glorious day with crystal-clear skies and moderate trade winds taking us home. The air was cold and brisk, and we talked football while bundled up in sweaters, rubber boots, and foulies. Marc and I drank coffee. John drank cocoa. Marc had somehow kludged together a set of foulies using a discarded tarp from Tikehau, half a roll of duct tape, and other random pieces of cloth treated with various canned chemicals from the engine room. He was pleased with the results.

It was perfect Hawaiian winter weather—a spectacular cold-front storm followed by three or four days of magnificent clear days.

Invigorated, we once again honored Eric Hiscock and went to work scrubbing down the entire boat and tackling a couple of mechanical issues. We had to change out the engine glow plugs because the engine was getting slow to start.

Mauna Loa

21

Hawaii Landfall

W E MADE LANDFALL at sunrise on December 22 when we were 45 miles from South Point, Big Island. The 13,679-foot peak of Mauna Loa was snow-capped.

We stared in awe of the glory of that mountain. Marc mentioned how far off-shore the slope must be where it intersected the ocean floor, and then each of us pointed to where we thought that might be. That was a mind bender.

The wind went light as we approached South Point, which indicated that we were in for a weather change. We should have had blazing wind flowing down the Ka'u coast. We ghosted into the lee of the Big Island and slowly worked our way along the South Kona coast in beautiful night-time sailing conditions. At night on the Kona coast a cold wind flowed down from the mountain top, and we carried a 5–10-knot offshore thermal breeze all the way to Kealakekua Bay, where the wind dropped to zero. We decided to just drift and enjoy the serenity.

We got some much-needed sleep, as we had not slept much in the last few days while anticipating landfall. At sunrise, we jumped in to clean the bottom and prop and then carried on north.

The diesel tank ran dry, so we put in the last 10 gallons from the jerry cans, bled the engine, powered up, and motored to the pier in the town of Kailua-Kona. That was a shocking reintroduction to the World—lots of people, cars, and boats. I called the Honolulu office of U.S. Customs and Immigration to check in. The immigration agent, who did not sound like Inspector Clouseau, welcomed us home and asked that we check in again by phone when we got to Honolulu.

There was no fuel facility at the dock, so we walked up the hill to the Shell station that sold diesel for 70 cents per gallon. We also had to buy some 90-weight oil for the transmission. John and I made two round-trips, each carrying two 5-gallon jerry cans, while Marc tended the boat.

As we were returning from the second trip, we noticed the wind had suddenly gotten up and Marc was struggling mightily to keep *Lille* off the concrete face of the pier. Even though we had deployed several fenders, we suffered some minor damage to the starboard rail amidships, our first and only ding of the voyage. The wind was wrapping around the point and into the bay. We quickly jumped aboard and cast off, with the help of some talented bystanders.

We intended to sail directly to Honolulu, but rounding the point north of Kailua-Kona we ran smack into a 30–40-knot buster. Now what? We had a decent chart of the Big Island, and it showed a small harbor at Honokohau, broad on the starboard bow. I didn't know anything about the place. It was either that or plow ahead into the maelstrom and sail to windward 35 miles further up the Big Island coast to Kawaihae Harbor. Sailing across the Alenuihaha Channel in those conditions was out of the question.

Honokohau was then only a small basin blasted out of the lava. (It was enlarged a few years later into a comfortable and snug harbor with excellent facilities.) We motored in and saw a man waving for us to come alongside his boat. He was a big fellow with long white hair and a huge white beard, wearing BoonDockers and overalls that were too short for his long legs. He introduced himself as Roy Fox and his little trimaran as *Hihimanu,* Tahiti-moored in the fairway.

Roy told us to drop a bow anchor and back down to moor up on his starboard side. Marc passed him a coil of ⅝-inch line, and we dropped anchor in the fairway and started backing in alongside *Hihimanu.* Roy bounded ashore and secured the line to a boulder. As I maneuvered the boat, John said, "Roy, give me a stern line." Roy responded, "You want a stern line? I'll give you a dang stern line—if you ever come sailing into my harbor again looking like some fancy-shmancy yachtie, I'll…"

Then he busted out in the loudest laugh I have ever heard. The sound busticated off the rock walls. We had sailed all those thousands of miles in a very successful search for interesting people and then found the World's Most Outrageous Human right in Hawaii. It was hard for us to focus on mooring the boat, but we finally stopped laughing and got rafted up alongside *Hihimanu.*

What a wonderful welcome. Almost immediately several people from other boats came aboard. It was a tight little community of friendly folks. There was a French dude named Peter, who had recently sailed up from Tahiti. When we said that we had sailed up from Tikehau, he asked if we knew the boat *Jacques-Louise.* We told Peter that we had met *Jacques-Louise* in Bora Bora and had later seen them in Tikehau. He then smiled and asked if the boat name had changed. That was a good one. He obviously knew Jacques well.

We also met Don and Anita, who had recently moved ashore after their trimaran was blown onto the bricks on the Kona coast. They invited us to join them and all the others in the crowd for Christmas dinner at their house. We said that we had hoped to be in Honolulu by Christmas and would have to depart early the next morning to make it. That got a good laugh out of the group, and then Roy said that we should just hunker down where we were for a few days, let the winds calm down, and spend a pleasant Christmas on the Big Island. Actually, reaching Honolulu by Christmas would have been a challenge anyway since it was already December 23rd.

Roy and Peter had dinner on our boat. Roy brought a bottle of rum. Peter brought a batch of hot and spicy rice & beans which was perfect for the cool winter night. Roy kept us laughing, but I couldn't stay awake and that old feeling of having *Lille* snugged safely away in a calm harbor consumed me. Marc informed me the next day that Roy told outrageous stories well into the wee hours by the light of the main saloon kerosene lantern.

I woke up to the sound of Roy bounding around on *Lille*'s deck in his Boon-Dockers and overalls (he called them "overhauls" and kept his teeth in the top pocket along with three pencils and a micrometer). He announced: "If I find out which one of you Seagoing Cockaroaches cold-cocked me last night, I'll come after you and just watch out!"

Then he bellowed out his wonderful laugh. I looked over to the saloon table and saw the guilty party—an empty rum bottle.

The wind had gotten up even more than the previous day, but because Hono-kohau Harbor was blasted out of the lava rock, the 10–15-foot-high side walls provided shelter from the wind. The air was brisk.

We helped Peter change a flat tire on his beater Ford station wagon and then we all drove into Kailua-Kona, met up with Don and Anita, and had a hamburger at an out-door restaurant. That was the first real hamburger in many months. While in Papeete, we had tried to be complimentary of the hamburgers the restaurants offered, but they just weren't up to par. Roy's girlfriend Grace joined us. Grace was a beautiful elderly Hawaiian lady who spoke Hawaiian as her primary language but also spoke English. Grace reminded me of the beautiful Tahitian lady at the Bora Bora fruit stand.

Corky, a gentleman at an adjacent table, overheard our conversation about the sailing up from Tikihau and joined us. Corky and his boat had been rolled 360 in a hurricane the previous summer and he was preparing to depart for Somewhere South later in the spring. We told him that we were rather good at finding Some-where and met up with him later on our boat to study the charts.

I found a pay phone and called my family in Alabama and some friends in

Honolulu. They all said some version of "Oh, we are so glad that you are finally home." I could have but did not respond, "Not yet, we still have to cross that monster Alenuihaha." No reason to tempt fate and cause any more concern.

It was Christmas Eve, and fortunately one of the grocery stores was open, so we went shopping for a cookout at the harbor. Roy had set up a tent and grill. Lots of people showed up for hot dogs and beer. After the meal some of us boarded *Hihimanu* for an almost-full-moon cruise (the moon was full on Christmas Day). The wind had clocked a bit to the east, so we stayed in flat water and moderate winds within the lee just south of Keahole Point. Roy howled at the moon and told more outrageous stories. We got back to the harbor well after midnight and while mooring the boat, Roy tripped and fell into the cockpit and cut his forehead. We cleaned him up and put on a butterfly bandage—no big problem.

After waking, I made a big pot of Special Navy Fuel Oil and took the pot and mugs over to *Hihimanu*. The sky was crystal clear, and the air was cold. Perfect Hawaiian winter weather! Roy and I had a fine conversation about his life in the Pacific. He had spent the last 40 years in the Pacific islands and islands of Southeast Asia. He loved the Philippines. I agreed, having spent a lot of time in the Philippines while in the Navy.

We boarded Peter's station wagon and Roy's truck, and drove to Don and Anita's home for Christmas dinner. Grace prepared a huge meal of Hawaiian dishes, and we watched several hours of TV, took hot showers, and talked. It was a very special Christmas Day. We had to repair a flat on Roy's truck and headed back to Honokohau. What is it about cars with flat tires in Kona?

The weather gradually improved during Christmas Day, and we got ready to depart on the next afternoon. We told Roy that we planned to sail the rhumb line to Honolulu, but he recommended that we work our way north along the Big Island coast as far as the winds allowed and then bear away to a reach across the Alenuihaha. We changed the oil and oil filter and cleaned the fuel filters, got *Lille* squared away, and departed at 1600.

Roy had decided to accompany us up to Kawaihae or as far as conditions would allow. *Hihimanu* had a 15-horse Johnson outboard that moved the boat right along, towing her dinghy on a long painter. Roy had two handheld CB radios and gave us one so that we could continue our conversation and his outrageous stories. That was something completely new and different. The winds were light all the way up the coast, and we eventually pulled alongside *Hihimanu* to return the radio and

Roy and *Hihimanu*

said *Aloha* to Roy. He howled at the moon and bore off.

When we got back to Honolulu, I called Don to relay to the Kona crowd that we had made it and to thank them for the hospitality. Don told me that Roy had fallen overboard while motoring back to Honokohau and had somehow climbed into the trailing dinghy, pulled the dinghy up to *Hihimanu* hand over hand, and got to the helm just in time to prevent *Hihimanu* from piling up on the rocks. It was just another day at the office for Roy.

We were abeam Mahukona Light at midnight and bore away to a broad reach in perfect conditions. Go figure—we had 15–18-knot east-northeast wind in 3–5-foot seas, extremely unusual conditions for the Alenuihaha. Thanks to Roy's good advice, we had a magnificent sail all the way across.

We decided to take a break and visit the island of Lanai again. We pulled into Manele Small Boat Harbor at 1500 and got a slip. We were most definitely living well. We hitched a ride up to Lanai City and had a good visit with Charlie and Mabel Kealoha, whose daughter Pua had sailed with us to Lanai on our first inter-island cruise. They drove us back down to the harbor and came aboard for a while.

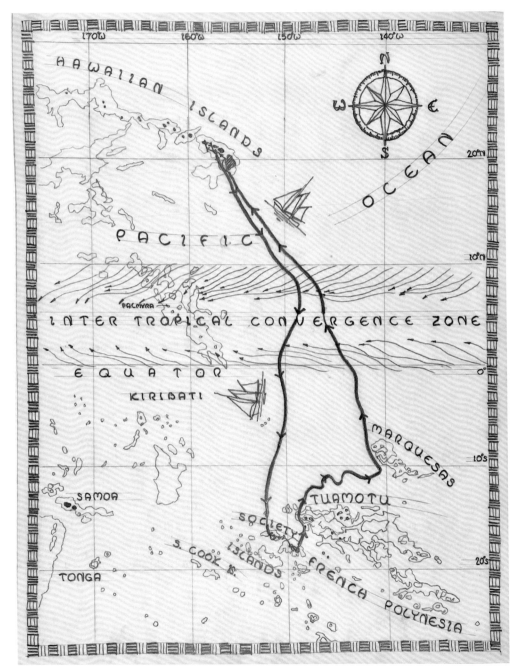

The big picture of the voyage

22

Back to the Real World

WE DEPARTED for the final leg to Honolulu the next morning at 0620 in light southeast winds, which gradually dropped to zero and we had to motor. A pod of spinner dolphins played on our bow wave with one young buck bracing his tail up against the stem to get pushed along. At 1300 we shut down and went for a swim and heard humpback whales singing. It was apparent that none of us really wanted the voyage to end—any excuse to prolong the good times.

One of Marc's crazy sky-diving buddies buzzed us in his twin engine Queen Air a few times. On the last approach he was below mast height and very close to our shrouds. He had seen us while he was returning from a charter flight to Maui. A little later we were dozing on the deck when my Navy buddy Roger Hammer, flying a twin-radial-engine Beach 18 affectionately referred to as the "Bug Smasher," made a sneak approach just above the waves and came within a few feet of us. Loud as a freight train, it scared the dreet out of us. Love the sound of those radials. Roger was on the return leg of a cargo flight to the Big Island.

We carried on and passed the time by cleaning the boat. When we were abeam Koko Head, a mother and baby humpback surfaced just off the bow, and we had to steer around them. We were certainly getting the royal welcome.

We arrived at the Ala Wai Small Boat Harbor sea buoy just after sunset, checked over the engine, prepared the anchor for deployment, motored in, and made up to the guest dock across the street from the Ilikai Hotel. We got *Lille* squared away, sat down in the cockpit, and looked at each other. Now what? There was no conversation. We had no idea what to do next. Where were the naked dancing women and how come we didn't have a Promenade?

Roger lived on his boat in the harbor and had gone over to Craig Fostvedt's boat, and the two of them came aboard with a bottle of dark rum and a bag of ice. Even though they were no match for naked Tahitian women, it was great to see them, and that kind of snapped us out of our lost feeling. Roger wasn't on the flight schedule for the next day and Craig didn't have class the next day, so they stayed well past midnight bringing us up to date on the news. Elvis had died, a couple of guys named Steve had started a fruit company, the world's population reached 4.3 billion. Nothing had happened in Hawaii.

I had a good sleep, awoke refreshed and made a mug of coffee, and sat in the cockpit trying to recap the voyage. No luck. We were back in the big city with traffic noise, people coming and going, planes flying overhead, and general brain-messing commotion. John and Marc came topside just when Roger showed up with his girl-friend Audrey and suggested we walk over to Eggs 'n Things, the best place in the neighborhood for breakfast. They had an early-bird $1.99 special of three pancakes and two eggs to order. While we were eating, Audrey pulled a 2-inch-long piece of blue-vinyl-coated #14 copper wire out of her scrambled eggs and said, *"WHAT IS THIS?"* Deadpan and right on cue, Marc pointed to Audrey's scrambled eggs and said, "Them is eggs and that there is a thang." Marc had developed a decent Illinois version of redneck-speak.

John called home and learned that his father was very ill, so made flight arrangements to leave the next day. I called a friend who had been driving my 1972 VW Squareback and he brought it down to the harbor. While driving to the air-port, John and I discussed selling the boat and agreed that it was the logical thing to do, since neither of us would be doing much bluewater sailing anytime soon. *Lille* was a bluewater boat and should not be harbor-bound. And of equal importance, we had to get back to the reality of earning a living. Things were moving way too fast, and it was hard to focus.

I posted flyers on the harbor bulletin board and put the word out amongst friends in the sailing community. I was able to find a temporary slip within the harbor, and during the next few days Marc and I got the boat emptied of all the extraneous gear and provisions and scrubbed down the inside thoroughly.

I was also able to find a slip at Makani Kai Marina in Kaneohe, so a few days later, Marc and I had a fine sail around the windward coast of Oahu in moderate trades. Once abeam Makapu'u Point, we were able to crack sheets and reach off. We put out the last of Uncle Odie's lures and caught a nice mahi mahi. We sailed into Kaneohe Bay and put *Lille* to bed. That made the voyage full circle.

During John's absence I painted the interior of the boat and put down some nice carpet in the main saloon. A friend offered to make new seat cushions for the settees and bunks, and that really spiffed up the place. I took the three working sails to a loft in Honolulu for a once-over. The sails didn't need much work, but it was reassuring to know that they were sound and ready for the next voyage. I cleaned

Kaneohe Bay

the engine, touched up the paint, and changed out all the hoses and belts.

John's father improved and John returned to Hawaii. As time allowed during the next few weeks, we worked to make *Lille* a showpiece. Marc had started working for a diving company that had a contract to scrub the underwater hulls of Navy ships. Even though he had a busy work schedule, he showed up to help as often as possible. Marc was especially good at varnish work and took pride in producing a perfect finish on all the topside brightwork, including the doghouse, rails, masts, and booms. He spent a lot of time up the masts, and I noticed him sitting on the crosstrees a few times just staring out to the ocean. I wondered if he was thinking about going back to Mareva in Tautira.

Lille was gleaming throughout, and I know she felt proud. She was in better shape than she had been on departure day. We had honored Eric Hiscock to the end.

23

Bon Voyage, *Lille*

JOHN AND I were sitting in the cockpit after finishing our work one day when another hopeless romantic showed up and fell under *Lille*'s spell. He had seen the flyer on the bulletin board at the Ala Wai Harbor. It was pitiful. The poor guy was done before he even stepped aboard. Marc showed up with a 12-pack of Olympia beer. We polished off some of the beer and talked with the fellow for a few hours about our voyage and his sailing experiences. The guy had done a lot of sailing and obviously knew his stuff. He had long dreamed of sailing Somewhere South. It was our mutual good fortune that he had found us.

Later, after he had made an acceptable offer to buy the boat and had departed, *Lille* and I shared a couple of beers and a few memories and had a long discussion about the future. She said that the buyer seemed to be a decent chap and would take care of her, so she was okay with him, but was worried about me. I told her that I would be just fine as long as I knew that she was getting out into the open ocean regularly.

Contrary to the adage that the happiest days of boat ownership are the day you buy the boat and the day you sell the boat—the day we sold *Lille* was not a happy day, and I still miss her. In my opinion, the happiest day of boat ownership is the day you cast off the docklines and sail out into the Big Blue.

EPILOGUE

Look around me
I can see my life before me
Running rings around the way it used to be
I am older now
I have more than what I wanted
But I wish that I had started
Long before I did
And there's so much time to make up
Everywhere you turn
Time we have wasted on the way
So much water moving
Underneath the bridge
Let the water come and carry us away

from "Wasted on the Way" by GRAHAM NASH

I HAVE SPENT 40-something years thinking about what the voyage meant and what we learned. We were extremely fortunate to have the time and the means to do something that some might consider to be a frivolous diversion from the realities and responsibilities of life, but we became better humans for having made the voyage. We learned the metaphorical life lesson of casting off the dock lines and forging out into the unknown. We also learned the meaning of hard work by confronting situations in which taking immediate action was not optional but essential for survival. In severe conditions on a sailboat, one must often do tasks that would otherwise seem to be beyond one's strengths and abilities. Those tasks sometimes must be done without full consideration of the consequences.

Don't get me wrong. What we faced was nothing compared to the difficulties experienced by sailors of old, especially the Polynesian voyagers and those who sailed the square-riggers on the grain route between Australia and Europe.

I recently reread Alan Villiers' terrific story *By Way of Cape Horn*. Every single day of his five-month voyage was more challenging than any one day that we experienced.

Lille Dansker was the perfect boat for our voyage in 1977. We were primarily out there for the adventure, and we couldn't have chosen a better vessel for three novices to learn the ropes. I especially enjoyed the gaff-ketch rig—so much to learn about how it was done in the old days. We enjoyed the demanding work required to sail a heavy-displacement vessel that had very few modern rigging systems that make modern boats more efficient and easier to sail.

What is a boat? Non-boaters might think that boats are inanimate objects much like a household appliance. Any serious boater will tell you otherwise. Every proper vessel is a living and breathing being with a defined life and purpose, a personality, an appreciation for the ocean environment, and a need for a devoted and worthy crew that allows her to explore open water. *Lille* had all of that and had the personality part in spades—she could be a caution and kept us constantly wary of her next surprise.

A boat must be pretty and must feel good about herself to perform and to do what she is meant to do. *Lille Dansker* was certainly a lovely thing, and she knew it. I admired *Lille's* confidence whenever we approached a new island. She sailed into each new location with head held high and chest out, proudly announcing her arrival in a new anchorage.

We developed a better appreciation for the natural world and the importance of being not just occupants but responsible participants as well. David Attenborough's excellent documentary *A Life on Our Planet* described his awakening and revelation after seeing the first photo of Planet Earth taken from the Apollo spacecraft in 1968. He stated: "We are ultimately bound by and reliant upon the finite natural world about us." He was able to put into words what we were just beginning to learn during the voyage.

The ITCZ is a fascinating place, and I have enjoyed several more voyages through that confused and constantly changing environment.

Electronic charts are now replacing paper charts, with good reason, but I believe paper charts should be carried on all cruising boats. (They will soon be collector's items.) I am old school and find that poring over a paper pilot chart provides a good "big picture" of the proposed voyage. Anyway, that was all we had for planning in 1977. Nowadays, voyage planning accuracy has improved significantly with several excellent programs. Subscribers can log in via satellite to download near

John with mahi mahi during sail from Fiji to New Zealand, 2016

real-time weather forecasts and receive recommended weather routing that takes into account desired departure date and time, forecast wind and sea conditions, and vessel performance parameters. These programs also provide recommendations for avoiding undesirable weather conditions. I now utilize those services as a matter of course, but still bust out and study the pilot charts (although it must be said that the validity of historical data assumed by the pilot charts is coming into question as the climate changes).

We learned a lot about human nature and that the common denominator of people everywhere is the desire to be happy and respect and care for one another. My Navy experience had programmed me to adhere to rigid schedules and defined goals. Polynesians are not as concerned about schedules but are certainly healthy, productive, and happy people, who put great value in caring for and considering the opinions of others. While we were still young and naïve when we completed the voyage, we had learned enough to realize that we had a long way to go.

John married Rhoda, and then earned his MBA from the University of Virginia and enjoyed a successful banking career in Charlotte, North Carolina. He is retired now and spends a lot of his time in Hawaii. He sailed with me in Tonga in 1994 and again in 2016 from Fiji to New Zealand.

Marc crashed his truck while driving down the long and winding road between Wahiawa and Waialua, Oahu, two years after the *Lille Dansker* voyage. He did not recover from the injuries. I joined a group of his sky diving buddies in a helicopter to spread his ashes over Mount Kaala in the the Waianae Range and over the ocean that he loved. I will always remember Marc as the quiet guy who went at life full throttle and would try anything without hesitation. He was a perfect shipmate, and I am honored to have known him and sailed with him. He lived on the edge during his short life, and he was an inspiration. This world needs more men like Marc. I hope Marc is living in Paradise in Mareva's valley.

I met Gail during a sail offshore Waikiki aboard a 50-year-old Alden schooner. We married and she got me squared away. I had an interesting and rewarding career in the marine construction industry which allowed me to devote a good part of my time to projects on and under the ocean. Over the years, I managed to take time away from the office to race and to make numerous ocean crossings. I also continued service in the U.S. Navy Reserves until retirement as a Deep Sea (HeO2) Diving Officer, commanding the Reserve Detachment of Mobile Diving & Salvage Unit One, Pearl Harbor.

I corresponded with Ah-Ki by mail and sent him some photos taken during our time with him. In 1985 I sailed a 38-foot sloop to Papeete. Gail flew down to join me and we sailed down to Bora Bora. We found Ah-Ki at his house. He greeted us with "Aloha Ya'll." Gail is always good about arriving with gifts and presented Ah-Ki and Teraii with macadamia nuts and Kona coffee. We stayed for dinner, and the fascinating conversation resumed as if I had never left. They were both doing well and never stopped smiling and laughing.

Ah-Ki insisted that we use his new Vespa motor scooter and provided detailed instructions for the fuel-shutoff valve: "Maybe you go—turn like this. Maybe you stop—turn like this." We practiced manipulating the valve a few times to meet Ah-Ki's rigid specifications and then drove the Vespa down to the new restaurant, called Bloody Mary's, for dinner. On the way back to Ah-Ki's, we stopped at the Magisan Chin Lee for supplies. The following day Ah-Ki took us in his canoe out

Sailing with my family in Fulaga Island, Lau Group, Fiji, 1994

to his *motu* where he and his daughters had established a very productive papaya and citrus plot. We also stopped by the Bora Bora Yacht Club and said hello to Alex. His yacht club was a big success.

Before flying home from Papeete to Hawaii, Gail and I took *Le Truck* to Tautira. Gail told me that she had doubted my glowing description of Tautira village, but when we arrived, she said that I had understated the beauty of the place. We found Pirae at his house. Mutoi was there. Our 1977 group photo was on Pirae's window ledge.

While doing some research for this book I learned that Capt. James Cook anchored in Tautira Bay, during his first voyage to Tahiti and the bay is often referred to as Cook's Anchorage. During his second voyage to the South Pacific aboard *Resolution* and *Adventure* the ships were bound for Tahiti from the Tuamotus. Cook came on deck on the morning of August 15, 1773, in light airs to find that *Resolution's* Officer of the Deck had allowed the ships to get dangerously close to the reef near Tautira. Both ships grounded briefly but were able to get free, losing three anchors in the process. It had always been assumed that the anchors

My sailing buddies in Whangaroa Harbor, New Zealand, 2016
Clay, Gail, Noodle Leary, Blossom and Kana and Mark Logan, Tom Gannon, John

were lost in Tautira Bay, but in 1978, the year after we were there, English movie director David Lean *(Lawrence of Arabia, Dr. Zhivago, Bridge Over the River Kwai,* etc.) was in Tahiti scouting locations for a movie about *HMS Bounty.* He chartered Rodo's boat *Vaite* to survey the uninhabited shores of Tahiti Iti. During the surveys, Lean's special effects director, Eddie Fowlie was busy conducting extensive research and study of Cook's logs. He was a mariner and a logical man and after analyzing the data, he concluded that the anchors had been lost not in Tautira Bay, but near the pass to the East of Tautira peninsula. Working out of a Boston Whaler with Rodo at the helm and a renowned local diver named Charlie, they found the Bower Anchor from *Adventure* in 106 feet of water spot on right where Fowlie had calculated. Awesome and almost unbelievable! A subsequent operation recovered the anchor. In 1979 David Lean produced a short film entitled *Lost and Found—the Story of Cook's Anchor* about finding and recovering the anchor. It is a very entertaiing film and shows Rodo driving *Vaite* and the Boston Whaler.

In 1994, Gail and I sailed the South Pacific for a year with our son Jonathan (10) and our daughter Grace (7). It was an unorthodox but rewarding education for all of us, something that we will cherish forever. Jonathan and Grace developed into independent and responsible citizens of the world.

During a sailing visit to Bora Bora in 2008, I learned from Ah-Ki's daughter that her father had "ascended" shortly after building a fine family complex.

The *Lille Dansker* voyage taught me the importance of a congenial crew. Sailing competence is certainly valuable, especially in trying conditions, but like everything else in life, a good attitude can endure and thrive in the worst conditions. Over the years, I have been fortunate to sail with excellent crew on every ocean crossing on my own boats and as crew on boats owned by friends. Some of the best crew members have been total sailing novices who have come aboard shouldering a seabag packed with a great attitude, enthusiasm for every minute, and a cheerful approach to tackling demanding situations. Gail has a pleasant attitude about sailing. Like most people, she doesn't really enjoy difficult sailing conditions, but she is a good sailor, stands her watches, and makes sure that the social atmosphere onboard is always comfortable, the conversation is interesting and educational, and everyone feels that his or her position on the boat is important and valued. You know a crew is working well together during a voyage when the cockpit conversation is rarely about sailing, but about subjects that one might have never considered.

Sailors are always looking for the perfect boat. Each of the boats that I have owned had individual qualities that made them handsome and fun to sail. I learned to appreciate the advantages of a fast boat, but not just for the thrills. Speed adds a margin of safety to a passage. Even more important than speed is simplicity. Always thinking about the ultimate simple boat, I appreciate this quote from L. Francis Herreshoff: "Simplicity afloat is the surest guarantee of happiness."

I am looking for my next boat. Life goes on.

PHOTO AND ILLUSTRATION CREDITS